Guitar

Guitar

*Playing with David Bowie,
John Lennon and Rock and Roll's
Greatest Heroes*

EARL SLICK
with Jeff Slate

MICHAEL  JOSEPH

PENGUIN MICHAEL JOSEPH

UK | USA | Canada | Ireland | Australia
India | New Zealand | South Africa

Penguin Michael Joseph is part of the Penguin Random House group of companies
whose addresses can be found at global.penguinrandomhouse.com

Penguin
Random House
UK

First published 2024

001

Copyright © Earl Slick, 2024

The moral right of the author has been asserted

All images courtesy of the author except: Chapter 4, © Ann Limongello/Disney General Entertainment
Content via Getty Images; Chapter 5, © David Lichtneker / Alamy Stock Photo; Chapter 10, © Ullsteinbild /
TopFoto; Chapter 11, bottom, © Everett Collection Inc / Alamy Stock Photo; Chapter 13, © Brian Rasic/
Getty Images; Cover photograph by Denis O'Regan

Set in 13.5/16pt Garamond MT Std
Typeset by Jouve (UK), Milton Keynes
Printed and bound in Great Britain by Clays Ltd, Elcograf S.p.A.

The authorized representative in the EEA is Penguin Random House Ireland,
Morrison Chambers, 32 Nassau Street, Dublin D02 YH68

A CIP catalogue record for this book is available from the British Library

HARDBACK ISBN: 978–0–241–37170–1
TRADE PAPERBACK ISBN: 978–0–241–37171–8

www.greenpenguin.co.uk

For Michael Kamen

Contents

Foreword

By Noel Gallagher

I first noticed Slick at Glastonbury 2000. He was playing with Bowie. What astonished me was how many styles and genres this guy could cross and morph into something uniquely his own.

From R'n'R to Jazz, from Pop to Punk, from Funk to Funky, and all that mad angular shit that doesn't even have a genre but Bowie was famed for. How could one guy do it all? I left Glastonbury that night thinking the guitar gods were not dealing these cards out evenly and that Bowie was a very lucky boy and that maybe one day I could find a guy like that to play for me. I'm STILL looking for that guy.

NGX

On stage with David during the 2003–2004 Reality Tour.

Prologue

'You don't look so good, boss.'

David was ashen and drenched in sweat. He'd stopped singing altogether as we wound up the song 'Reality', a favourite of mine off the new record. We'd only been on for about half an hour. It was blisteringly hot on stage. Barely any air. But something wasn't right. We all felt it. You could see it in the faces of the crowd. David's eyes caught mine as he hunched over.

Fifteen thousand pairs of eyes staring at us melted away as I called over to the side of the stage where David's security guy, Nick Belshaw, stood watching, his expression a picture of concern. In a flash, Nick rushed him offstage. I didn't know what was going on, but I knew it wasn't good.

We soldiered on with a couple of tracks without him – 'A New Career in a New Town', 'Be My Wife' – before David managed to come back on stage. We played a few more songs. Nick brought him a stool. After the first few chords of 'Changes' he couldn't continue. David always gave everything to a performance. Some nights he'd even come offstage and puke in a bucket from the exertion.

But this was nothing like that.

Up until that point things had been going really well. We were about to wrap up the biggest tour David had ever embarked on, and everybody was in great spirits. The Reality Tour had been gruelling but fun, too.

It was my fifth outing with him over the thirty years since we first played together on the Diamond Dogs Tour, and we were working our asses off, especially David. But it was one of the best times of my life, and I think that was true for David, too. He seemed happier and healthier than I'd ever seen him and relaxed in a way that he'd never been before with the band and the crew, and most especially the fans, who greeted us with a rapturous welcome everywhere we went.

By the time we hit Prague, the band had played over one hundred shows since the tour began on 7 October 2003 in Copenhagen, Denmark. Over nine months we had criss-crossed Europe and America through 2003 and into 2004, before heading to Asia, then back to the US, finally winding up in Europe again.

After David left the stage in Prague, we got back to the hotel in short order. Not hearing shit, even from the tour manager, Frank Enfield, I started to worry. When I caught up with Frank later, he looked serious and that was my first tip-off that things might be worse than anyone was letting on. Frank was normally an easy-going guy. He said an ambulance had taken David away but assured me, 'Everything is going to be okay.'

I raised my eyebrows and gave him The Look. That's when he told me David had a 'blocked nerve'.

'What the hell does that mean?' I asked. I'd never heard the term before.

Frank shrugged and said, 'Be ready to head for the next gig.' We were due to play in Hamburg, at the Hurricane Festival, two days later, on 25 June 2004.

At first things seemed like business as usual in Hamburg, although I couldn't help wondering about David's health. The dressing room was damp and cold. Outside, a downpour had turned the outdoor arena into a typical German mud fest.

Backstage, David was sitting in a chair with his eyes closed. He looked like a bat the way he was all folded up. He'd been sitting there for a while, real quiet, and he sure didn't look himself.

'You okay, boss?' I asked him.

'I'm not feeling great. Maybe the rain,' he mumbled, waving me off. He didn't make eye contact and it seemed as though he could barely talk.

Everybody was quiet. There was none of the usual goofing around, or the bullshit the band and David typically engaged in to get our collective energy up before a show. But when it was time, David got up, as if strings had pulled him to his feet, and headed for the stage, followed by the band: Mike Garson on piano, Gerry Leonard on guitar, Gail Ann Dorsey on bass, Sterling Campbell on drums, Catherine Russell on keyboards, and little ol' me on lead guitar. After playing so many shows, we had become an unbelievably tight unit and knew what to expect from each other on stage. As I took my usual spot to David's right, I got a weird vibe in my bones. As the show wore on, I found myself keeping an eye on him, not to watch for the usual musical cues, but just to make sure he was alright.

He was sweating again, like in Prague, and his colour had drained away. But you know what really threw me? David was wearing an oversized, taupe hoodie. Now, David was a super-stylish guy and his onstage outfits were put together with all the precision of a Mercedes-Benz, every aspect meticulously engineered months in advance down to the stitching. So, to see him in the spotlight dressed like he was going to the gym was just bizarre.

As the show wore on, I found myself transfixed by his hoodied frame. I barely looked at the audience. He always felt larger than life once he got onstage, but that night he seemed to get smaller and smaller. And he seemed to be going through the motions, which for a consummate performer like David was highly unusual. About halfway through the show, I saw him rubbing his left arm and his chest. And yet, by the time we got to 'Heroes' he managed to hit his stride. It was a killer performance, one of the best of the tour. 'Heroes' always made a connection in Germany, the place where it was conceived and recorded. But still, I sensed, as the song wrapped up, that in his mind he was already making his way to the tour bus.

As the last notes of the encore rang out, David smiled that warm smile of his, but it faded quickly as he bowed. I heard him exhale a big, exhausted breath as he made his exit. He didn't look at me or say a word as he passed by. He kept walking and disappeared backstage. I glanced at Gail, who was on David's other side, and her eyes locked with mine. All of us looked around at each other as we waved to the cheering crowd, our eyes darting from one to another, acknowledging that something was up.

By the time we got offstage, David was nowhere to be seen. As the crowd thundered their approval, little did I realize that this would be the last show he'd ever perform. Or that following heart surgery he would slip away from the public eye completely. Or that I wouldn't see him again for eight years until the car I was driving caught fire and some local news crews reported the incident. The next thing I knew, I got an email from David asking, 'Are you okay?'

Pretty soon, what he really wanted became clear. 'What's your schedule like?' he asked.

Getting started. Practising in my bedroom after being inspired to pick up the guitar by bands like The Beatles and The Stones.

I

No Expectations

I got bit by the rock-and-roll bug when I was thirteen years old.

Seeing The Beatles on *The Ed Sullivan Show* was something that you can't understand if you didn't experience it first-hand. I know people study it, but they can't grasp the impact. The Beatles weren't a band. They were a goddam gang. Since the 1950s, it was mostly one guy or a group like The Everly Brothers with a backing band. Even the girl groups, like The Shirelles, later, were backed by a band. Now, all of a sudden, and for the first time, you had a completely self-contained unit. No backing band. No extra guys on stage making that sound. It was *them*. They were playing their instruments and doing all the vocals themselves. The outrageousness of Elvis, Little Richard and Chuck Berry had gotten my attention, but they'd been basically put in their place. Not The Beatles. The Beatles came along and picked up the baton and said, 'Fuck you, you can't tell us what to do.'

I was born Frank Madeloni in Brooklyn on 1 October 1951. My earliest memories are of the radio blaring because my grandmother always had it on in our kitchen; all these hit songs floating on the airwaves, mixed with the aroma of her cooking. This was in the 1950s, so I'm talking about Bobby

Darin, Ricky Nelson and Johnny Mathis. A lot of the later doo-wop stuff floated around, too, but that wasn't what I gravitated to. Of course, there was Elvis. I *loved* Elvis.

Besides the music on the radio, I remember little bits and pieces beginning from about the first grade. By then I was living in Red Hook, Brooklyn, in a six-storey walk-up, and it seemed like half the people on our block were related to me. It was a tight-knit Italian neighbourhood, with a lot of interplay between extended families.

Later that year, we moved to East New York. My father bought a house on Staten Island. By that time, I'd discovered television. I watched these crazy cartoons where little mice ran around and this guy named Farmer Brown chased them. The cartoons were in black and white, and played this demented classical music as the soundtrack. They played that type of music in the Catholic school I went to, called St Sylvester's. It came through the public address system in the school. We would march upstairs from the schoolyard, up the stairs to our classrooms to this goose-step music. It was heavy duty. So that was my introduction to classical music. I remember it, though. I remember that music.

At about that time, I started to key into popular music on the radio. None of my friends shared my interest, except for one kid, so we became pals. But I was never the guy that would hang out in a group, anyway. I did not like group activities of any kind. Organized things, like Boy Scouts and the rest of that shit, made me uncomfortable. Still do. It wasn't as though I felt like a freak. I didn't feel anything about it. I just did my own thing, on my own.

Meanwhile, my mother, unbeknownst to me, was suffering from severe depression and would almost never get out of bed in the morning. I'd get up and dress myself, make my own breakfast and put my lunch together to go to school. I did the same thing for my little sister, who was a few years younger than me and not even in school yet. Not realizing the condition that my mother was in, it all seemed very normal.

And then, there was this girl. I was still in the first grade, and she must have been in the seventh or eighth grade. Back then there were no junior high schools, so we all just mixed together. We'd walk home from school together because we lived on the same block. Sometimes on the way back from school, we would stop at her friend's house, which was maybe a block from our house, and we would go down into the basement, with its black-and-white tiled floor, where the girl who lived there had a record player going. That was my introduction to rock-and-roll music. Man, do I remember that. I'm not sure why that girl and her friends tolerated me, but I really enjoyed the hell out of hearing Elvis, Chuck Berry and whatever else was current at the time.

Eventually, after that high, she'd drop me back off at home. My house was a beater. It was an older house, built in the late 1800s; a two-storey, single-family soapbox house like Sears sold. In fact, that place was in such bad condition that there was one room in the house that I didn't even go in because the plaster was coming down and you could see the boards behind it.

My dad didn't have the wherewithal or money to fix it

because he was busy changing jobs at the time. He had worked for the Transit Authority as a bus mechanic until he got hurt. It wasn't bad, but he ended up going to the Police Academy because being a cop paid more, even though he was twenty-nine, which was old at the time for that.

One day during the summer after first grade, out of nowhere, ambulances pulled up to the house and my mother was taken out and put into one. That was in 1957. I was six. And I didn't see her again at all for an entire year.

Within twenty-four hours, I was shuffled off to my grandparents' house in Crown Heights, Brooklyn. Remember the EF Hutton commercial? 'When EF Hutton talks, people listen'? Well, that was my grandfather. He didn't say shit, but when he said something, you fucking listened.

My grandfather was a bit flash. He kept weird hours and had a brand-new car every year. In those days, that was unheard of. I found out later he owned a pool hall. Nobody ever gave me details, but knowing that, I'm sure he was up to no good. He would arrive home from work in a perfectly pressed suit, tie and fedora, and shoes you could see yourself in like a mirror.

Meanwhile, my grandmother was really great. Her kitchen centred the house, and it was where I spent most of my time because that's where she basically lived, and that's where she had her radio.

I was going to public school, but the only friends I had were not from school. They were two Italian kids from the block because my neighbourhood was a heavy-duty mob area at the time. I still didn't see my mother, and my father maybe visited me once or twice the whole year I was there with my grandparents. But I don't remember being an unhappy or discontented kid. I was fine.

Eventually, my mom got out of the hospital, my dad got an apartment in Sheepshead Bay and I moved back in with them. I loved it there, even if I wasn't very fond of the school, mostly because of a park across the street that had swings, handball courts and trees, and one of those sprinkler pools that only another New Yorker from that same time period will ever have seen.

That whole time in Sheepshead Bay, I don't really remember much music. If that had been the seventies, it would have been a different ball game. Music would have been everywhere. But because I grew up in the late fifties and the early sixties, in Brooklyn, New York, I didn't know anybody that played anything. Nobody did.

Elvis-mania was over by then. The only stars we had were the ones that came out of Disney's *Mickey Mouse Club*, Frankie Avalon and so on. I didn't pay a lot of attention to them.

My dad, through his partner in the NYPD, bought the house in Staten Island in 1962, which was two years before the bridge opened, so the houses were affordable. That was the only way he could have managed it because there's no way he could normally have bought a house on a cop's salary, even back then.

The big mystery was how the hell my grandfather loaned him the extra money he needed. My grandfather had something going on, definitely. I remember the amount of money my dad borrowed because to me $2,000 sounded astronomical. My grandfather had that cash in his pocket to give my father when we went over to see him, for a house that cost him $15,600.

Meanwhile, my parents couldn't afford to put me in a Catholic school. That was a huge relief. Thank God for small favours. I sure didn't miss those nuns. I spent a good part of the sixth grade dealing with bullies and getting into a whole lot of fights. Even then, I wasn't afraid of anybody. Nobody taught me that. I just wasn't. I had no fear.

Because I was new, and because everybody hated anyone from Brooklyn, I didn't have any friends and was on my own a lot again. But we had one of those Emerson stereos with a TV built in, a record player and a little compartment for LPs, and my mother, who was back home, played a lot of music. She would go out and buy records. Mostly, she played Patsy Cline, Hank Williams and country records. The hits. Chet Atkins, too. I remember him vividly because his instrumental guitar records knocked me out.

And then I saw The Beatles on *Ed Sullivan*.

John Lennon was the guy I could relate to. He was a dark figure. Soon enough, Brian Jones and Keith Richards came along too and things got even darker. In short order, I became a Keith fan because when I saw him on TV, playing those Chuck Berry licks, it knocked me out and made me get serious. Up to that point, I hadn't made any decisions or had any real conscious thoughts that I was going to play guitar for a living. After seeing Keith, it just happened. I never thought about it more than just playing the guitar day and night. I didn't have any agenda or anyone telling me I could make it or I couldn't make it or that it was crazy reaching for the stars. It never occurred to me. The inspiration Keith provided deep down was what drove me.

I watched the guys in my neighbourhood who were already playing. They were only a year or two older than me, but that was a huge gap, especially when you're beginning to play an instrument, and especially back then. Pretty soon I knew I was getting a lot better than all of them, really fast. That really sparked me on.

When I was sixteen, I joined my first band. We weren't bad. We could play, but we were too young to even sneak into bars. We ended up playing these underage places because there were plenty of those, and high-school dances because those seemed to happen every week.

By the time I turned seventeen, I had started my own band. Finally, we could make money because we were old enough to play in bars. The drinking age in New York was eighteen, but we had fake IDs. That band, Mack Truck, was just a bunch of guys from the neighbourhood. We were friends who stuck together and I thought of us as a gang, like The Beatles or The Stones, but we were young kids with limited life experience, so it was more like a high-school football or baseball team. Because we were all in it together, we lived and breathed the shit twenty-four hours a day. Pretty soon we started to get jobs, and they were good jobs, making really good money.

It had only been four years since I'd seen The Beatles on *Ed Sullivan*. I was driven enough to stay on it, but there was still no conscious thought to it, either. I just did it. I'd get up in the morning and it was all I thought about and all I had. I still didn't have any aspirations or thoughts about being rich or being a star or 'look at me'. I wasn't thinking 'I want to play The Fillmore', where I went to see shows all the time. I never thought about anything other than what I was doing in the moment back then because I just loved playing. That focus got me to another level.

I'd met some guys that shared my love of the blues, and the same style of American rock and roll and British blues that I was into. A couple of them came from Staten Island like me, and the singer, Jack O'Neill, who came from Boston, had ended up living in Florida as a kid and had the blues thing down. We would sit and talk about Muddy Waters and Bo Diddley, Jimmy Reed and Solomon Burke; heavy stuff considering we were only seventeen years old.

Jack looked like a frontman. Rock and roll is about the look as much as the sound. I look at photos of back then and I still think, 'Damn, we had it going on'. He was absolutely a great frontman and a hell of a writer, too.

So, me and Jack – who's still around – got really close. We called our band Beau Jack, a name he came up with after a not very well-known prize-fighter from the 1920s. It was the perfect name because it was 1968, and we were doing a hardcore blues and Stones thing. Pretty soon it got red hot.

In fact, that's where my stage name, Earl Slick, originated. Beau Jack was doing five nights a week, four sets a night, and working that hard made us all pretty crazy. And Jack, being a natural frontman, would often kill time telling stories and giving us goofy, made-up names when he would introduce us. And with Jack being from Florida and me being from Brooklyn, he absolutely loved to make fun of the way I talked. Well, one day a ship busted open and spilt a bunch of oil in New York Harbor. It was all over the news, and when I got to the club that night I couldn't wait to tell the guys what I'd seen on *Live at 5*, the must-see afternoon news programme at the time. 'Man, you wouldn't believe the oil slick,' I said excitedly. Meanwhile, Jack was just about falling off his chair, though I couldn't understand why. The more I went on about it and the more excited I got, the more he cracked up. Finally, he stood up.

'It's oil slick! Not earl slick!'

Huh? Whatever, dude.

Well, that night, after a big wind-up, when Jack introduced the band, he introduced me as Earl Slick. The crowd went wild and, to be honest, I kinda loved it.

In fact, we all loved it. So it stuck. I've been Earl Slick ever since.

When the British Invasion thing happened, with the screaming girls and all, I was into it, but knew that wasn't my scene. I started digging into the blues world. All of a sudden, the Yardbirds and Cream and Hendrix happened, and exploded what R&B and the blues could do. I already knew the masters – Buddy and Muddy and Jimmy – but Beck and Hendrix and Clapton were doing it electronically, with fuzz tones and out-of-this-world chops.

Of course, I didn't have any of their tricks. I was just learning the ropes, playing a Telecaster through my first Marshall 50-watt half stack with an 8 × 10 cabinet. But pretty soon, I moved on to the big baby: a 100-watt Plexi. Man, I wish I still had that.

In 1968, everything was happening around me. I was in

New York playing all the time. Drugs and sex and music were flowing. Bands like Traffic, the Jeff Beck Group and Sly and the Family Stone played every night at places like the Academy of Music and the Fillmore East. I was drinking all that in while playing my guitar every chance I could. When that guitar wasn't in my hands, I showed up everywhere I could, trying to make connections.

Eventually, through a mutual friend, I got the attention of a guy named Michael Kamen, who'd just finished up at the Juilliard. He'd started a rock band where he was mixing a little bit of that Juilliard classical training with a rock thing. The New York Rock & Roll Ensemble was winding down by the time I hooked up with him, so he'd gone out on his own. He was a hustler, but trained and serious about the business, and we hit it off right away. He produced some demos for my band Mack Truck and was generally looking out for me. Whenever an audition came up for something he was working on that he thought I was right for, he'd call me in. That's how I auditioned for the legendary New Orleans piano man Dr. John at age eighteen. Nothing ever got released from those sessions, but playing with the late, great Mac Rebbenack was one of my first real professional studio gigs.

I was also developing a sound of my own. I'd acquired a cherry-red Gibson SG and a Fender Telecaster, but the big Marshall Plexi amp I had was holding me back. I'd become a pretty steady customer of Larry DiMarzio's, one of the best luthiers in Manhattan. He worked at Eddie Bell's guitar shop, and I would take my guitars there for repairs and whatever. And as the relationship grew, I would talk to him about the gigs that I was doing and how I kept getting fired up because I didn't really like to use fuzz tone pedals, and while I wanted my amp to break up as much as the next guy, because I refused to use anything smaller than a 100-watt Marshall I was just too damn loud for everyone before I got any distortion out of it.

One day, he said, 'I can do something with the pickups that might help break that amp up a little bit quicker.' He took the pickups out of my SG and he rewound them to make them sound fatter and louder.

I did a lot of gigs back then – even before working with David Bowie I was doing four or five gigs a week in the early seventies – so because there was healthy competition, a lot of the other guitar players came to see what I was up to, and they were knocked out by my guitar sound. I got questions about how I was getting the sound and I told them, 'This guy, Larry DiMarzio, he's really got this down.'

Over time, Larry started doing the same modifications for other people. One thing led to another, and eventually he figured, 'Why am I doing this? I should be making my own pickups.' And that's what happened. He never looked back and DiMarzio pickups were born.

I was learning the Rules of Engagement for how to act in a recording studio, because you've got to remember your place in the pecking order when you're at the studio. Most of all, you've got to remember to shut your fucking mouth and listen to Dr. John or Michael Kamen or whoever is talking. When they ask you to play, you play. When they ask you to stop, you stop. And you shut up.

I was also still playing around the old neighbourhood, taking anything I could get. You name it, I was doing it, hustling my butt off, and learning a lot in the process. Of course, by that time I knew how to handle myself onstage.

Rock and roll was in my bones, and I knew it was in my bones and that this was what I was gonna do forever. This was my life. I was never going to get a job. I wasn't going to go to college. None of that shit. I knew how to take care of myself because I'd been doing it since I was six years old, when my mom had been AWOL due to depression and I had to fend for myself and take care of my little sister.

Meanwhile, we were going through managers and producers, working and cutting demos. We were in and out of studios because the studios sent talent scouts out, and they'd get the record companies to cover an afternoon for you to go in on their dime and record as many songs as you could. Then you'd sign a piece of paper that said they had six months to say yea or nay. After six months, you'd get your songs back. That's what we were doing. But we got frustrated as hell because we weren't getting signed.

In 1971, we hauled ass out to the West Coast for a while. I hated it. Los Angeles had no edge to it. Not like New York. I told our drummer Jack Mack, aka Claude Pepper, flat out, 'Fuck this shit,' and came back to New York after a couple of months. But Jack and his brother Jimmy, the lead singer, stayed there.

I rejoined the rest of the band in the configuration that was playing gigs. They were doing schmaltzy covers – Crosby, Stills & Nash songs – and they wanted me to learn the three-part harmonies. I needed to work, but eventually it dawned on me. This ain't fucking Muddy Waters. This ain't The Rolling Stones. This ain't Willie Dixon and Chuck Berry. Fuck this shit. This music is for fucking pussies. If I continue this, I am going to still be here when I'm thirty. An old man.

I went to see my friend Hank DeVito, who played pedal steel guitar and went on to become a very successful songwriter in Nashville. He wrote that song 'Queen of Hearts' and a lot of country hits. At the time he was in Michael Kamen's new band, along with David Sanborn on sax and Dennis Whitted, from the Paul Butterfield Blues Band, another favourite of mine. I wanted to be in that band!

I asked about it and Hank said, 'Michael doesn't need two guitar players, but if you want to come out and haul the gear, you could do that.'

I thought, 'Why not?'

These guys were touring, playing everywhere from the Northeast to the Midwest, flying there, staying in hotels. It was the real deal. To me, in that moment, that was big time. In my mind I thought, 'Okay, I can get the hell away from Staten Island and I don't have to play this garbage with these guys anymore. We'll see what happens. In the meantime, I can get drunk and chase girls around and have a good time.'

Of course, in short order, and because I did bring my SG with me, I ended up jamming with the band during soundchecks. One day David Sanborn turned to Kamen and asked, 'Why isn't he playing in the band?' And Michael looked at me and asked if I wanted in.

'Of course I do!'

'Okay,' he said, 'you can play in the band, but you've still got to carry the gear.' That was fine by me. This was my first real 'show biz' break, and I have David Sanborn, who became a lifelong friend soon enough, to thank for it.

We were doing original tunes that Michael had written. Some were local hits from his former band, the New York Rock & Roll Ensemble, and the rest were from his first solo album, titled *Michael Kamen*, which had just come out. The music had a rock edge to it. It sure as hell wasn't the Stones or anything, but the calibre of the players made all the difference in the world.

Anyway, it didn't matter to me what it was. It was rock music, in its own way, and it sure wasn't that syrupy shit I'd been playing. I was happy being there and certainly not worried about what was going to happen next. I was thinking, 'Okay, this is cool,' not 'I'm going to parlay this into a better gig so I can get on the path to becoming a rock star with a million dollars.' I don't think like that. I was playing music and I was getting paid. That wasn't something a lot of my friends were able to do. But I was. So I enjoyed it. Every minute of it.

In between Michael's tours, I'd get back to Staten Island and get Beau Jack or one of the hybrid bands I had going on together and we'd do some gigs. I was hustling my ass off because those bands weren't only playing on Staten Island. We were playing up and down the whole Greenwich Village circuit.

The scene was broken into three segments. One segment was all these guys doing perfect cover-band stuff. Then there were guys doing cover-band stuff that was edgier, mixed with their own material. And then there were bands playing only their own stuff, though that was the minority. I had a band that was in that minority. We were good. We came really close. But we never did get signed.

As much as I was enjoying life, there's no getting round the fact that I'd been treading water for a while when Michael called me up in early 1974 with news that would change everything.

'I think I've got an audition for you with something that's pretty serious,' he said. I already had a reputation for being a wild card, but Michael's standards were high and he must have also thought I was good enough by that time. I asked him who it was, but he wouldn't tell me.

He said, 'Look, I'm not at liberty to say anything. Just get your shit together because I'm going to call you again in a couple of days.'

And that was when I found out David Bowie was looking for a guitar player.

Celebrating with the late, great Michael Kamen. Michael's early support was critical to helping me break into the industry.

2

Hello Spaceboy

RCA Studios in 1974 featured lots of brown and beige and shag carpeting. Everything did in those days, but studios, which were dark all the time with no windows or any way to tell what was going on in the world outside, seemed to double down on it. RCA was no exception.

When I got to the giant midtown studios, just off Sixth Avenue, I was shown past two mean-looking security guards into a small room with some amps inside what seemed an almost empty building. When my eyes adjusted to the dark, I made out a small, stylish woman with curly brown hair standing there. She introduced herself as Coco. That was it. No surname. I looked around and saw no one else there. The glass window to the control room was completely black, peppered with little red monitor lights. Like something out of *2001*.

'This is fucking weird,' I thought. I expected the audition Michael Kamen had hooked me up with to be with a band, so to walk into an empty studio, with just a couple of amps and some woman who I'd never met, was really strange.

Coco and I chatted for a bit. Small talk, really, but I could tell she was sizing me up to gauge how I was reacting to the situation. I tried to take it all in my stride. I plugged in my Gibson SG to the Marshall Plexi and double stack amp I'd requested and set about getting some sounds.

Finally, from behind that jet-black control room glass, a voice crackled through the studio monitors asking me to put on a pair of headphones on a nearby stool. Forget *2001*, this was more like *1984*. I did as I was told. The instructions came with a New York accent. Whoever it was giving the orders, it sure as hell wasn't David Bowie, the man I thought I was there to see.

There I was, in an empty studio with nothing but my guitar and an amp, facing the glass window into the control room, talking to a disembodied voice. *What the fuck?*

'We're gonna play you some tracks, just play along,' the voice said.

Up to that point, the only David Bowie album I'd owned was *Aladdin Sane*. I'd heard songs like 'Panic in Detroit' and 'Watch That Man' and I loved the guitar sound and playing of Mick Ronson, David's guitarist and foil throughout the Ziggy Stardust years. But that was all I really knew about David's music. Listening through the headphones, I immediately realized that these weren't songs I knew, but I knew I could still dig my teeth into them without any problem.

'Hang on,' the voice from the control room said. 'I'm going to open up some space for you to play.'

When the playback started again, the guitar was gone. I had to scramble and find the key, then improvise, right there on the spot. I later learnt the first song was called 'Diamond Dogs', and I loved it. It was right in my wheelhouse, so I dug in and went to town.

After fifteen or twenty minutes playing to tracks that I'd never heard before, the music stopped and the studio went silent for what seemed like forever.

'Hello?'

'Give us one second.'

Then the door opened and in walked David Bowie.

Jesus.

Man, he was skinny as a rake. And pale. He was dressed the way an English rock star might think a Harlem pimp would dress. Loose, baggy pants matched with Capezio dance shoes. It was a weird combo, but very cool, too. And I was especially struck by the way he moved. He was graceful for a rock-and-roll guy. To top it off, he had bright orange hair under a grey fedora. Then, as he got closer, I noticed he didn't have any eyebrows!

Whoa. Up to that point, I'd only ever seen David on TV, in magazines or on album covers. Each time, he'd had a different look. In person, he was even more striking. Unnerving even, because *he didn't have eyebrows* and was just beyond skinny.

David was definitely the strangest cat I'd ever seen, and I'd been around some off-the-wall characters, even at that point in my career. Still, within about five minutes I felt really comfortable. However off-the-wall he looked, and however much of a star he already was, I liked David right away. And I could tell that this was going to be fun.

I'd turned up in a red velvet jacket – with a flask of brandy inside one pocket and a vial of speed in the other – and jeans with a giant belt buckle and boots on, plus hair down to my ass like Cousin Itt from *The Addams Family.*

But David was cool with me right away, despite our totally different vibes. He had a warm smile on his face, so I broke out the brandy and we had a swig and a smoke as we chatted.

'I like the way you played,' he said. 'Where are you from?'

'Brooklyn.'

I realize now that he was grilling me to find out what I was about, but at the time it felt easy and comfortable. At no point did David put his cards on the table – he didn't then and he really never would with any of the guys who worked with him – but despite the reserve, I didn't find him intimidating or stand-offish either. I liked him from the get-go.

At the same time, even though I didn't have all that much experience with artists of David's calibre at that point in my career, I realized that he'd set things up so that if he didn't like me, he wouldn't have to look me in the eye and tell me himself he didn't want me for the gig.

It was an important lesson in dealing with David that I never forgot: he never, ever went to anybody personally to give them bad news. Either somebody else did it or it didn't get done at all. In that case, you would just realize one day, 'Funny, I haven't heard from David in two years.' So, I learnt early – that first day, in fact – that David always wanted to keep himself separated from anything personal, difficult or uncomfortable. That's just the way he was. He never, ever wanted to have to be the bad guy. And he'd made sure he didn't have to be.

After we'd chatted a bit, David picked up a guitar and we started playing together. It was loud and fun, and we both loosened up a lot. David wasn't a great guitar player, but he had a truly unique approach that took him in directions a more seasoned guitarist wouldn't always think to go. He'd developed his style as a way of expressing the songs in his head. As a result, he used a combination of made-up chords and distinctive strumming. It got the job done, but it was totally different from the way a guy like me, who played in a more traditional, blues-based style, would do things.

It was really cool that night in RCA Studios, but I've got to admit I wasn't paying that much attention to it. I was just playing and I wasn't fazed. I mean, I wouldn't say I was cocky, but I was certainly borderline. The truth is, I was just being me. I knew he was a big deal, but from where I stood, why should that change who I was? I think it counted in my favour.

We played the song I'd played along to from the beginning again. David sang over the top and his voice was full and absolutely unique, with perfect pitch. I became a total fan of David's in that moment.

'What's that one called?' I asked.

'"Diamond Dogs",' David replied. 'It's new.'

'I dig it,' I said. 'It's got that Stones thing going on.'

'That's funny, because that's what I was going for,' he said. 'But I don't think it turned out sounding anything like The Rolling Stones.'

'Well, maybe we can have fun with it live and turn it into the song you wanted it to be,' I said.

Pretty quickly, I caught myself. 'Shit,' I thought, 'that was ballsy.' I hoped I hadn't overstepped the mark, but David laughed and we kept playing.

Whew.

Pretty soon I could tell David was done. He got up, with a big smile on his face, and after some charming banter, he made a beeline for the door. And that was it.

I started to pack up when Coco showed up again.

She said: 'We've got about a dozen more guys we're going to see over the next two weeks.'

'Cool.'

'We'll be in touch, okay?'

'Sure,' I said. What could I say?

This was in the days of payphones, so I got to the corner and called my buddy Hank DeVito to come pick me up. Then I started to get worried; I thought I'd blown it. The audition had started around nine and it was only eleven. Maybe I *had* been too cocky. Hank showed up and I was pretty quiet on the ride back to the neighbourhood. I was relieved when we pulled up to the Swiss Chalet in Great Kills, Staten Island, the little blues bar that was our home away from home.

Once I'd realized who the mysterious audition was for, I'd told Hank. I couldn't help it. But I swore him to secrecy because if I didn't get the gig, I figured I'd be hiding in a hole for a while. But he'd gone and told everyone we knew.

When we walked into the bar, the whole place let out a big cheer and started clapping. *Motherfucker!*

I was pissed. Especially as I was starting to feel pretty sure that I didn't get the gig, and now everyone was going to know. I played it cool, and let my pals buy me drinks, but I was seething inside.

I slept in the next day and was woken up by my phone ringing incessantly.

'Goddammit,' I thought. 'Don't these motherfuckers know if I don't get it on the first few rings, I'm not going to get it?'

I stumbled over to the phone and when I picked it up, ready to give whoever it was a verbal beating, I recognized Coco's voice.

'Earl?'

'Yeah?' I croaked. I was hungover and I hadn't even had my first cigarette yet.

'David was really happy with what you did yesterday and would like to know if you'd like to join him,' she said. 'Can you come to David's suite at the Sherry-Netherland this afternoon?'

'Sure,' I said, trying to play it cool. I still didn't feel certain about things, but this was definitely a good sign. It hadn't even been twenty-four hours.

The Sherry-Netherland was one of the fanciest hotels in New York City. It stood right across from the Plaza Hotel, on Central Park South, with a big, beautiful clock on the façade. You've probably seen it in a million movies.

I walked in that afternoon, surrounded by the gold-leaf Louis XIV and French provincial furniture everywhere in the lobby, and took a look around and thought, 'If David is inviting me to his room, he must want to hang and talk.'

When I got up there, I was stunned. It was the biggest hotel room I'd ever seen; a two-bedroom suite the size of a football field, it seemed, with gleaming white walls and a white grand piano in the corner by a window that looked out on the Plaza.

David was nowhere in sight.

There were people hanging around, doing this and that, and a little boy, who I learnt later was David's son, playing with a lovely woman named Miriam, his nanny, but I tried not to get too distracted. Coco showed me to a big ornate white couch, and I sat down and waited.

At first, I just sat there, but as time dragged on everyone started to make small talk. It turned out Coco Schwab was David's assistant, and she was really cool. Everybody else was great too, and we had a lot of laughs, but I got anxious as time went by. After an hour, Coco told me David was sleeping.

'Of course he is,' I thought. 'He's a fucking rock star and it's the middle of the day. Of course he's asleep.'

I chuckled under my breath and tried to relax.

Eventually, the sun started to go down and only then did I sense some movement coming from behind one of the bedroom doors.

And then, there he was. David Bowie. He was wearing a crisp white T-shirt, and the same brown Capezio shoes and grey fedora as the day before, with a pair of baggy, drawstring pants that were stylish as hell. I looked at them and knew immediately they weren't any sweatpants. They looked expensive. I wanted a pair!

We began to chat, and he offered me a beer. I sensed that I was there because he wanted to have a second look at me and that he was feeling me out, but it was still very relaxed.

'Look, this is what we're doing,' David said. 'We've got

some rehearsals coming up and then we're hitting the road for most of June and July. Then we'll probably be out most of the autumn. I'll get you the details later, and I'll make sure somebody gets you the material you need to learn.'

'Sounds good,' I said. 'But listen, how close do you want the guitar to the original stuff; the Mick Ronson parts?'

'You're Earl Slick, you're not Mick Ronson,' he said. 'I like what you do. Do what you do. Do what you feel. Just play the way you played last night and I'll be happy.'

Man, that was a relief. I was worried I was going to be expected to copy Mick Ronson note-for-note, and I'm not very good at verbatim copying people's parts. I mean, I could have emulated Mick's style because I thought he was the quintessential sideman, and I still do – but note-for-note? I was a little concerned that the fans were going to want to kill me, but that turned out not to be the case. I was even a little bit nervous for the first gig replacing Mick, but fuck, I got great reviews on my first show, so happy days, as they say, but I'm getting ahead of myself.

After a little while hanging out together, I headed home. I was excited because I learnt that my buddy and mentor Michael Kamen was the tour's musical director, and that my old buddy David Sanborn, the ace saxophonist from Michael's band, was also in the line-up. I was sure it would be a great band and a lot of fun. Plus, David was a star on the rise. It really doesn't get much better than that for a sideman, which after years of trying to make my own thing happen, was what I realized I was. For now at least.

A couple of days later, Coco called me to tell me David wanted to hang out again.

Okay, back to the Sherry. This time there were more people buzzing around in David's suite – Coco, Miriam, David's son and Angie, his wife at the time – plus some hairdresser friend of his named Jack. David sat me down and without much being said, Jack came over, pulled his scissors out and got to work. Before I'd really had time to clock what was happening, my hair went from Cousin Itt to a two-inch crop.

I freaked out.

'I just joined a rock-and-roll band and you've cut my hair,' I said. 'You're supposed to cut your hair when you work in an office.'

David clearly sensed that I was about ready to bolt. He explained to me that the short hair was going to go along with a whole look he had planned for me and everyone in the band.

'You'll see,' he said, trying to reassure me.

Next, a seamstress friend of David's appeared and started measuring me up. I was wearing my street clothes and regular Joe shoes, but David explained they were going to make a two-piece, double-breasted 1940s-style suit, with a high waist and a short jacket.

Admittedly, it sounded kind of cool, but it didn't make me feel any better. I'm not sure which I hated more, the short hair or the fucking shoes I was told I was going to have to wear. *And* I was going to be wearing a suit? Now I really felt like I had signed up to work in a fucking office.

Pretty soon I was back out on the street, waiting for Hank to pick me up. I wasn't even sure he'd recognize me with my short hair. I couldn't wait to get back to our neighbourhood for a drink, even though I knew all my pals were going to rib me mercilessly about my new look.

Waiting there in front of the Sherry-Netherland, as the sun went down on a perfect spring evening in Manhattan, the greatest city on Earth, it dawned on me: 'Fuck 'em all.' I was about to head out on the road with one of the biggest stars on the planet, playing some of the coolest music being made at that moment. I'd put in my hours – and then some – before I'd gotten the fucking gig. I'd been playing professionally since I was a teenager, five nights a week for the past five years already, plus recording sessions. I was on my game and playing great, so I knew I had nothing to worry about there. And I felt pretty sure I was in good hands with David.

Now, I just had to get my ass ready for rehearsals.

On stage with David during the 1974 Diamond Dogs Tour.

3

Dogs on the Road

David had already pretty much finished *Diamond Dogs* when I got the gig. They were mixing it. David had played most of the guitar parts himself in the studio, but he was planning to tour and, without Mick Ronson, he needed a guitarist. What he wanted was a mouldable, hungry, younger player, someone who would be happy to be there, but also had the chops to pull the gig off. He didn't want a name that he'd have had to pay a lot of money. At least, that's my take.

I found out I only got that audition because of a quirk of fate. Michael had written some music for the Joffrey Ballet, and David had gone to the ballet and really liked the music and wanted to meet the guy who'd scored it. When they met, he said, 'By the way, you know a lot of guys around here, can you recommend a young guitarist or any guitar player? Because I'm looking for one.'

The only name Michael gave him was mine.

The lead guitar player in any band is almost always a pretty volatile person, and a lot for any singer to deal with, so I think it was a smart decision to get somebody who was still on the up. I was getting well-known in New York City, but that was it. That was inviting to him.

Now, I saw myself at the time as a straightforward, meat-and-potatoes rock and roller. I mean, Keith Richards was still my idol. Was then, and still is, but I also didn't feel like I was doing anything weird or out of the ordinary by going on the road with David because Mick Ronson was definitely part of the same school as Keith. It felt great because I was going to be able to just be me.

Now that I had the job, I didn't have any nerves, really. The funny thing is that the only time I got concerned was during the gap between the original phone call and the audition. But I was not that familiar with the process or, more importantly, David's music. I only owned one Bowie album at the time: *Aladdin Sane*. I loved Mick Ronson's guitar playing on 'Panic in Detroit' because it was souped-up Bo Diddley. And 'The Jean Genie' was built on a big blues riff like Muddy Waters' 'Mannish Boy'. I knew where *that* shit came from. I didn't know anything about 'Space Oddity' or 'Changes' though. I recalled having heard them on the radio because they were hits, but I hadn't paid any attention to them. We never played anything like those songs in my bar bands, as we weren't even aware of them. But *Aladdin Sane*? I really did love that record. I had to get familiar way beyond that one album though because I didn't know what the rehearsals were going to entail. I went out and either bought or borrowed every record of David's I could and started listening to them like crazy, learning every song.

Now I had the gig and I had a rehearsal schedule. David left me a setlist at his office, so I picked that up and went out and bought what I needed to learn all the songs: a whole bunch of records. I returned to my apartment with *The Man Who Sold the World*, *Hunky Dory* and *Ziggy Stardust*. I sat there in front of my record player with my guitar and just kept playing along with them, over and over again. I just learnt the song structures and as far as copying solos, I learnt the few with signature guitar lines. I wasn't trying to mimic Ronno or anyone else, but the lines crucial to the song, like the twangy bit at the beginning of 'Diamond Dogs', I got those down. And I really worked my ass off, so that by the time I got to rehearsals, I had the structure of the whole show together.

The rehearsals took place at a studio in midtown Manhattan. We had the whole band there 'routineing', or running through, the songs and the arrangements because Michael Kamen, who was the musical director under David's direction, took the original arrangements and reworked them. 'All the Young Dudes' is a good example. These days, David's demo, which he cut for Mott the Hoople, is easily available. But back then, we did not have a recording of it. We did our own take on it, based around Michael's guidance. 'The Jean Genie' started off with Herbie Flowers doing this slide thing on his bass, which was very different from the recording I'd been learning from. I had to start paying attention because I'd learnt the structures of the songs as they were recorded, however this did also mean it was easier for me to make the guitar parts my own. It was like learning completely new songs but with chords I already knew. And the songs changed as the rehearsals progressed. Because I'd worked with Michael before, it was easier. I understood Michael's MO. And he knew how to work with me. Even though I was young, and relatively green, having that rapport helped a lot.

There were lots of drugs around, but as I'd started young, it seemed like nothing to me. I'd been drinking from the time I was thirteen. From the first sip, I loved the way it made me feel. I felt self-assured. Even invincible. By fifteen, serious drug use had kicked in. I'd gotten a summer job at a fast-food place to help me save up for an amp I had my eye on, and the manager used to give us all speed – namely Black Beauties – on the weekends to help us through the twelve-hour days.

Later, when I was doing gigs, I started getting high and drinking even more. It had nothing to do with 'I'm in pain. I'm depressed. My childhood was terrible. I'm going to drink.' But I'd discovered that if I had at least a few drinks before a gig, it was a whole lot easier because I got hellacious stage fright in those early days. I couldn't look at the audience. The more I drank, the more I turned around. Then it became a lifestyle thing. It was just part of what I did and as much a part of me as my guitar was. The booze, the dope, everything. It was all-inclusive. That was me, in the same way that I dressed, the way I played, and how I faced the world with a 'fuck you' attitude. It was all me. It was what we *all* did, just like going out and getting a hamburger. It was no different. Part of the daily routine.

In those early days with David, at the rehearsals for the Diamond Dogs Tour, I always had a bottle – whiskey, wine, whatever – sitting next to my chair. It may have been afternoon, but it was completely normal. And even though I did a lot of crazy shit, it didn't affect my playing. Not then. At least not in the way it did later on. So, I'd worked my way up and had no trouble hanging with even the guys in the band who were really going for it.

Meanwhile, David was at all of the rehearsals. I would come to realize that this was unusual with other guys, but not for David. Through every period I ever worked with him, he was always at rehearsals, and always at sound checks. He had a work ethic and attention to detail that you didn't often see with people in his position.

The band had David Sanborn on sax, who, of course, had already worked with Michael Kamen, Herbie Flowers on bass, Tony Newman on drums, a baritone sax player named Richard Grando, Michael Garson on piano and Pablo Rosario, who was our percussion player and used to play with Tito Puente. We also had what they called 'the dogs,' who were Geoff MacCormack, aka Warren Peace, and a dancer named Gui Andrisano, whose wife was Margo Sappington, a Broadway choreographer. They sang backing vocals and did all of the dancing that went on during the shows. I was the only guitar player. Rhythm and lead. That was cool. Like Pete Townshend.

Amongst all these great players, having David Sanborn and Michael Kamen there was crucial for me because I'd worked with both of those guys before. Michael had already taken me under his wing and for somebody my age, that was a big deal. Getting reacquainted with David Sanborn, not to mention playing with him, was really important for me. He was the first sax player I'd ever played in a band with and if you're going to start off with a sax player, it might as well be David fucking Sanborn, right? Picking up where I'd left off playing with Michael's band, he and I would jam around at sound checks, and I picked up a lot of sax-type licks from him. We became good friends. Very good friends. Before we finally came to our senses, we got into a whole load of no good plenty of times during our time off and sometimes when we were working, to be honest. He was a pretty central part of that whole Diamond Dogs Tour period. A real partner in crime.

Herbie Flowers and Tony Newman came as a set having worked together with T. Rex. I knew of Tony because he had played on Jeff Beck's *Truth* album, but I was familiar with them both and I was awestruck by them because of the difference in our ages, which was ten years plus, and because they had that mentoring, big brother, teaching-the-new-guy-the-ropes thing going on. Being around them was like being in a fucking Monty Python movie. They were the two most irreverent fuckers you ever could imagine in your life, the sort who might take a garbage pail full of ice and beer and throw it out of a fourth-storey dressing-room window. They were these crazy fucking Englishmen, although Herbie was extremely business-minded, which you wouldn't think, given the way he and Tony acted.

Then there was Geoffrey MacCormack. He'd grown up with David and was an important part of the stage dancing and the background vocals, along with Gui Andrisano. Percussionist Pablo Rosario alongside the fantastic pianist Mike Garson, who'd joined up with David during the tail end of his Ziggy days and played the amazing solo on 'Aladdin Sane' was the icing on the cake. David had all these different personalities – a really great cast of characters – but there really wasn't a whole lot of drama going on, at least until the band expanded later on and things changed.

Aside from Kamen and Sanborn, I really liked Geoff. He was one of the only old friends of David's that I'd ever met. Even though we were all working together as a band, there was clearly a bond between the two of them that went back before all the fame. Because of that, he seemed to have an innate ability to do or say something so ridiculous that it would break the tension in half when things got tense. He could diffuse almost anything, which was appropriate given that Geoff went under the stage name Warren Peace.

A choreographer named Toni Basil choreographed David, Geoff and Gui, who between them acted out these vignettes that David had designed to help tell the story of Diamond Dogs. As far as the rest of us, it was just basic blocking. 'This is where you stand. This is where *you* stand.' That was it. That's all she did with us.

David worked us hard in rehearsals. But it was a great band, and things clicked right away. Best of all, he let me do my thing. Just me and my trusty '65 Gibson SG Junior, which I had bought in 1967 at Sam Ash on Kings Highway in Brooklyn, when there was only one Sam Ash. I'd paid $125.

I'd seen Clapton with an SG. He'd played a Standard, but when I started pricing them, they cost too much money. Then somebody told me about SG Juniors. I looked at a couple of them and fell for them right away.

I saved up the money and bought it. To this day, the SG Junior remains my favourite style of SG. But I digress. Guitar players and guitars, eh?

A typical rehearsal would run eight hours. We would usually start in the mid-afternoon and work into the evening. The rehearsals were pretty focused. These guys were the cream of the crop. They knew that no matter how crazy they got, that work was work, and so we all really focused on getting the arrangements together and everything.

That went on for around three weeks and David was there every day, with Michael Kamen making any corrections and changes to the arrangements and David okaying them as we went along. He left Michael to do his job because one thing that David did – always did – was to let whoever he hired do their job. Then, if a correction needed to be made, David would make the final decision. But that's all he would do. It was a really smart and efficient way to get the best out of everybody. He didn't have to be 'The Guy' and be hands-on, all day, because that's just too much, and that's why Michael was there, anyway.

Once the first run of rehearsals was over, we had a week off. After that, we headed to the Capitol Theatre in Port Chester, New York, where they had set up all of the staging, with the full 'Hunger City' backdrop based around David's *1984*-inspired apocalyptic vision, plus the lighting and sound. We had a series of full-on dress rehearsals over the course of about ten days.

The first time I saw his ideas for 'Hunger City' it was just a bunch of little cardboard cut-outs on a three-foot-square board. It looked like a little toy playset with tiny cut-out people and buildings. It looked totally fucking nuts. I'd taken the gig, number one, to play rock and roll. They'd already made me cut my hair off and wear a suit and old-man shoes. When I saw the mock set, I couldn't help thinking, 'Okay, what's going to happen next?' But during rehearsals, I kept my head down and did my job. But when I saw the real fucking thing, all built and imposing, even menacing, I literally said out loud, 'Holy shit.'

It was amazing. And unlike anything I had seen up to that point and, in some ways, ever since. I mean, the only people that were doing big theatrical shows like David was attempting were Kiss. But all they did was wear outfits and set bombs off. Whereas David had hired Jules Fisher, who was the go-to guy for putting together sets for Broadway, to build the dystopian 'Hunger City' set he wanted as the setting for the show.

The set had all these moving parts and was huge, with theatrical, Broadway-type lighting. When the audience walked in from the back of the theatre, they saw the façades of buildings and a moving bridge at the centre of the stage, which eventually David would get up on and that would move up on hydraulics while he sang 'Sweet Thing'. You couldn't help but be impressed. Plus, there was a cherry-picker with a seat on it and a telephone with a microphone in it, which would come down during 'Space Oddity' for David to sing in while he hovered over the first four rows of the audience, fifteen feet in the air above them. Pretty wild. To say David's ideas for a rock-and-roll show were ahead of their time is a gross understatement. The set wasn't just a backdrop. In essence, he envisioned a rock-and-roll Broadway show, with little vignettes in the show that carried the action along. During 'Panic in Detroit', David would box, and in 'Diamond Dogs', the background singers would tie David up with ropes. During 'Cracked Actor,' David did a Hamlet thing where he talked to a skull while he wore sunglasses and a red-and-gold cape.

All of those theatrics could have bothered me but the funny thing was, I was happy to be there. I was taking it all in and loving every minute of it. The thing that really got up my ass the most, still, was cutting my hair and wearing a suit. I didn't like that. The rest of it – once I got over the awe of seeing what it was all about and even though I wasn't a Bowie fan when I signed up – was really cool because I knew what he'd accomplished, and I was getting to be a part of that. I'd seen clips and photos of his Ziggy Stardust shows, so the idea that we were doing something like that was not really that shocking to me. Plus, when I was seventeen or eighteen years old, I'd been on the road in the backing band with some of the cast of *Hair*, so I'd been exposed to the whole Broadway mentality, and even back then I'd tried to just roll with it.

But mostly, I was happy for a big gig.

By the time we came out of rehearsals, I wasn't worried about a thing. The band was hot, the songs were great, and David was killing it. I'd never seen a frontman like him up close. He was mesmerizing. And his voice and charisma were off the charts. I felt pretty good.

You have to remember that with what was going on in the charts, and the other bands that were on the road at the time, like Led Zeppelin, Humble Pie and the Stones, this was a very different kind of show. We did stuff like 'Watch That Man', 'Rebel Rebel' and 'Diamond Dogs', which brought plenty of rock and roll to the show, but the tour was such an undertaking – with really elaborate staging and props – that I knew I was involved in something that had not really been done before and was going to have a major impact.

The only worry I had at the outset of the tour was once again trying to fill Mick Ronson's shoes. Despite David's reassurances that he wanted me to be me, it wasn't out of the question that the audience would hate me.

Performing with David on *The Dick Cavett Show* in 1974.

4

David Live

Right off the bat, on the first night in Montreal, we caused a hell of a ruckus. The audience went mental. What an amazing feeling to be part of that.

Now as I said, up to that point I'd had a few concerns about my role. When you've got an iconic band or artist, and you've got a key member of the band – like Mick Ronson was for David in Spiders from Mars, during his Ziggy Stardust days – it's a hard act to follow. There were only a few guys on stage, and they each had very distinctive roles and looks and styles. Mick Ronson was a striking performer and a striking-looking guy, not to mention being one hell of a guitar player. And here I was, replacing David's sidekick. His foil.

Oh my God, the fucking press and the fans are going to kill me, I worried. How can I take the place of this great-looking blond guy, who's already had as much exposure as you could have in those days? Mick had been all over television, and all over the magazines, and always had his picture in the paper with David. 'They're going to hate me,' I said to friends. The possible backlash stressed me out, until the reviews started to come in.

I didn't get a beating.

We followed Montreal with Ottawa and Toronto, and then Rochester, New York. What amazed me was the difference between rehearsing and being on stage looking out at 18,000 to 20,000 people. These were big venues, and every one of them had sold out. Before the mid-seventies, only bands like The Beatles, The Stones and The Who could do that kind of business.

Even as a kid, I was always the kind of guy that was never fazed by anything or anybody. But I was in awe of being in front of that many people and their reaction to what we were doing on stage. Before the first night, I thought I was prepared. But that night in Montreal, it hit me like a ton of bricks. Holy shit. This is serious fucking business here. But I got used to it really quickly. In short order – within the first week – it became the new normal, as they say. We were going to go do a show, and it was going to be pandemonium.

The reviews weren't all great, but they sure weren't what I thought they'd be. I really thought I was going to get killed by the press. I worried that if the reaction was awful, I'd get fired. If the press and the fans hated me, especially because they loved Mick so much, that would cost me my job. In my mind, not really knowing the history, I figured David could just get Mick back in the band if things didn't go well. But once I started to see the reviews, and the press and fans liked me, those worries went away. It was unnerving at first – more unnerving than having to learn the show – but I was flying pretty high once those first few reviews came in.

Meanwhile, playing to all those people every night, even

though it's David Bowie's show, started to mess with my head. I was standing up there. I was next to The Guy. I was playing guitar in front of 20,000 people. Mind you, after a month of intensive rehearsals, where we'd gone from just knowing the bones of the songs to them really taking flight, the band knew the songs cold. That's not to say we weren't nervous when the first few shows came around, and probably most especially me being the new guy. But pretty quickly, I went from worrying about taking the place of Mick Ronson – which is like stepping into Keith Richards' shoes as far as I'm concerned – to embracing my role as David's on-stage foil. Besides the backing singers, who moved all over the stage even though their moves were tightly choreographed, I was the only member of the band who was ever up front next to David. Even David Sanborn, who had a few sax solos here and there during the show, stayed in the back behind the massive stage set.

It was a thrill. Like any job, doing it day after day, it became easier and more natural for me. I'd get in the zone, everything around me would simply fall away, and I'd do what I was there to do. It just got better and better as the tour progressed.

And I watched David hit his stride as a performer. The show was so impressive that it pushed him up a pretty big notch on the A-list of rock-and-rollers. Not because the show was necessarily better than what those other acts were peddling, but because it was so different. And because it was doing so much business.

All of a sudden, it was Bowiemania. He was having to sneak in and out of venues, with fans going nuts outside the gates. It reminded me of the clips of The Beatles from the old days – like when I'd seen *A Hard Day's Night* as a kid, which was only ten years prior – with them getting chased down the street by fans. That was happening with David.

Coming from New York, I figured this show wouldn't play well down South. All the 'phobes are there, right? Anybody who saw somebody like David in America at the time might instantly think, 'He's gay.' Considering anti-Civil Rights shit was still going on back then, let alone someone coming across as gay, I was genuinely worried about what might happen. In his interviews, David would tease reporters and goad them with cryptic or snippy answers, or sometimes he would just manipulate them and make them look like complete fools, which he was very good at, of course. Back then, that wasn't too cool, especially down South. So, I was more than a little surprised that the people in quite a few conservative cities embraced the show the way they did.

But most of that barely penetrated our bubble as the whole thing was getting bigger and bigger. Pretty soon, David had bodyguards. In fact, we all had security. I wasn't a naïve kid. I could see that it was necessary and I figured this is what somebody does when they're this famous. They have these guys that take care of them, and protect them, and make sure that they're safe and the people around them are safe all the time. I didn't know any different and just figured that's how things were supposed to be once you got to that level.

As for life on the road, time ceased to exist. There was no such thing as daylight. I'd wake up in the early afternoon at some shitty Holiday Inn that David's management, Main-Man, had booked us into, quickly get myself together and just about make it down for the ride to the soundcheck. Then we'd eat whatever catering had put together for us backstage at the venue. Occasionally, some of the mechanics would go wrong because, like I said, David was so far ahead of his time in what he was trying to do. So maybe the bridge that rose out of the floor twenty feet in the air during 'Sweet Thing' didn't budge, or the cherry-picker didn't want to come down, leaving David hanging up in the air above the audience. Then, after the show and a long drive on the bus, where we'd drink and get high and play cards, we'd end up back at another shitty hotel in the wee hours, where a few of us would muscle our way onto the stage in the hotel's lounge with whatever local cover band was playing that night. Like this one time in Chicago at a place called Mother's, when we weaselled our way to sit in with whoever was performing by making sure they knew who we were before playing and blowing them off the stage. I can still remember the faces of those bands back then, as they realized we were in the big leagues and that they needed to step things up or pack it in.

Eventually, we'd stumble back to David's hotel, where there'd always be some drama going on outside of his room. You wouldn't believe the assortment of characters – groupies, drag queens, whatever – causing a ruckus.

Meanwhile, I was learning the ropes. Tony Newman and Herbie Flowers, one of the best bassists ever to pick up the instrument, were seasoned pros and friends who happened to work together all the time, so their camaraderie was infectious. I drank a lot with them. Tony and Herbie loved drinking and were always a blast to be around. I learnt a lot from Herbie, who was fifteen years older than me. I was in my early twenties and he was thirty-six, a big age difference, especially in the music business, where those years meant lots of miles and experience. Herbie really kept an eye on me, and became another mentor to me, just like Michael Kamen. When we got onstage, Tony and Herbie, but especially Herbie, would make suggestions and corrections to the way I was doing things, but always in the most positive, non-threatening way. Herbie's personality is very fatherly. But a nice dad, unlike my old man, who was either not there physically, or emotionally detached when he was around. Herbie guided me in a way that was not condescending. 'Oh, by the way, when we do this bit here, maybe you should try something like this.'

Except when it came to my shoes. At one point, we stopped using the costumes for a while because one of the trucks carrying the wardrobe had gone into a swamp in Florida. The driver had fallen asleep or something and ran the truck into a bog full of snakes and alligators. It took a while to extricate everything from there, and we did a few shows without our wardrobe, wearing our own clothes. We each had specially designed stage outfits, which at first we all loved, but soon enough we all hated. After the truck fiasco, I remember us all joking about it, David included. Because David didn't freak out about shit like that. He just wasn't a spilled-milk guy. He just went, 'Ah, shit. Okay. Guess what, guys? We're out of uniform tonight. Have a good show.' That was it. He wasn't upset at all.

I went out and bought what I thought was a cool pair of platform shoes. Herbie took one look at them and said, 'Those, my man, have to go.'

I thought I was being hip. It wasn't the way I normally dressed at the time, but I thought it would fit in with what David was doing. But no. Herbie nixed those. Can't pretend that didn't sting.

I took the rough with the smooth. After not too long, Herbie pulled me aside and said, 'You know what? You're a fucking star. People are going to know who you are for the rest of your life. You mark my words.' Coming from a guy who I looked up to so much, that really landed.

The tour was broken into two legs – two smaller tours, really – with a break for recording in the middle. The first leg of the tour had 'Hunger City' and lots of cool props and those amazing uniforms for the band. That first leg ran for about four months, mostly in the Northeast. And I felt completely at home on the road, right away.

I know lots of people complain about the road, but I loved the whole thing, every second of it, even though, back then, David would stay at a nice hotel and we would stay at really shitty Holiday Inns and whatnot. But it wasn't something I thought about much because I'd never done a tour of that magnitude. He was the star so, of course, he stayed in the nice place. I was just in the band. I thought that's how it worked. Some people on the tour were really bothered by it, and even though it didn't come from David, but from his office, David got blamed for it. But he was really good with people, and handled the ruckus well, I thought.

Except for maybe Radio City Music Hall, which came later, the most exciting part of the tour for me was the week of shows we did at the Tower Theater in Philadelphia, which is a great place to play. The performances were recorded and eventually released as the *David Live* album.

It wasn't free of drama, though.

During soundcheck on the first day, we were getting the sound right and rehearsing a bit. As we wrapped up, Herbie suddenly said, 'Hold on a minute. We're not done yet.' What I didn't know was that while we were doing our thing, he'd had his eyes peeled on something that was going on around us. Me, being a kid, I was oblivious. But Herbie wasn't a kid. He'd been around the block. And he'd noticed that, along with the normal sound guys rushing around, there were a lot of other microphones being set up, and he noticed them all leading to a truck out back. He saw that and put it together right away.

Herbie and Tony pow-wowed. After they talked, they came over to the rest of us. They'd figured out that management planned on recording the gigs, which typically they'd have to pay us extra for, except we didn't know anything about it. At that point, everything stopped and the band all headed back to our hotel. Sure enough, when I walked into my room, there was a contract under the door – with those little marks pointing where to sign – that said I'd get paid $70 for them to own the rights to a live recording of the shows. Forever. Almost immediately, Herbie called.

'Did you get anything under the door?'

'Yeah.'

'Rip it up. Don't sign it, okay?' And then he hung up.

Pretty soon we headed back to the Tower. Right away, I saw Herbie make a beeline for David's dressing room. I didn't hear it, but apparently a hell of a brouhaha went on in there. He told me later he'd told David flat out, 'Either we have an agreement on a fair price for everybody or we don't go on stage.'

It felt like MainMan had dumped this shit on David to deal with because they were nowhere to be found. And I'm pretty certain David had no idea beforehand of what MainMan tried to pull because, despite what I've said about him being the no-drama guy, when he found out he had a complete shit fit.

Herbie took it and then told him, 'Well, you know where we stand.'

In hindsight it was hysterical, but at the time it felt like maybe the gig wasn't going to happen, even though we were in the middle of a tour. But Herbie stood his ground – cool as could be – and he got David to agree. Even then, getting paid could be a pain in the ass. It seemed like Main-Man held on to our money as long as they could. Tony and Herbie weren't invited back for the second half of the tour, which I felt was a sort of subtle retribution for standing up for what was right.

But the shows were great, and my solo on 'Moonage Daydream' alone made my bones in the music business, so it's hard to have any complaints. Despite it all, the double LP *David Live* sounded good. Keith Harwood, who died quite young, bless his soul, was in the truck outside recording us, and did a truly amazing job. Those shows also marked the beginning of David's stronghold in Philadelphia. To this day, it is probably the place in America that has the most diehard Bowie fans. If you think about it, he recorded two iconic records in that city, because later we made *Young Americans* there.

I still run into people who attended the shows at the Tower Theater, and some were even at the recording sessions, or at least around the recording sessions, of *Young Americans*. For him to go to Philly – rather than New York, which is a stone's throw away, or LA or London – to record and make a live album was a big deal. The town is significant historically because of the Founding Fathers and all the history that they have there, but not as far as rock and roll is concerned. For him to embrace the City of Brotherly Love, with the amount of attention that it got for the city and the whole rock scene, was more than appreciated by the people there.

David was on truly top form, even if he subsequently said the album was 'Like vampire's teeth coming down on you,' and about the cover photo he said, 'My God, it looks as if I've just stepped out of that grave. That record should have been called *David Bowie Is Alive and Well and Living Only in Theory.*'

Maybe that's why the shows were never filmed properly. Over the years, I can't tell you how many people have complained to me about not having more than a few minutes of crappy black-and-white video and fan-shot home movies of one of the most talked about tours of the seventies. Setting aside how cheap MainMan was, let's face it, to film a show as complicated as we were putting on each night would have been more complex than what Martin Scorsese dealt with shooting The Band's *The Last Waltz*, which was filmed two years later. David was in a pretty bad place physically and emotionally in 1974. I'm not saying he wasn't on a creative roll. He certainly was, as history has proven. But between pressures from management and the demands he put on himself, not to mention the vampiric, drug-and-sex-fuelled lifestyle he was living, which to be honest seemed perfectly normal at the time, in retrospect it's a wonder he didn't crack under the strain.

David's growing interest in Philly Soul turned into *Young Americans*,
the first of his studio albums that I played on.

5

Soul Dogs

Back during rehearsals when David and I talked about my roots in blues and R&B, he lit up. I realized in an instant how important these were to him, too. He had a deep interest in artists like Wilson Pickett, Sam & Dave and all that seriously cool old-school R&B.

'Man, I love Eddie Floyd,' I said to him, 'I would love to do "Knock on Wood". I think it would fit right into the set.' He must have agreed because by the time we recorded *David Live*, it was part of the show. Its inclusion pointed the way towards his next change in direction. He just needed the players to help him.

By the time we wrapped up the first leg of the tour at Madison Square Garden, David was already talking about what he wanted to do at Sigma Sound, the studio that had been home to the Philly Sound and where a bunch of great seventies soul records were recorded. I'd already been in the studio with David to do overdubs on the *Ziggy Stardust* concert movie where Mick Ronson's rig had dropped out – yep, that's me in spots, not Ronno – but in Philly we really got to work, laying down the basic tracks for what would eventually become *Young Americans*. I played the signature acoustic guitar at the beginning of the title track. But the truth is, there wasn't that much for me to do. The solos belonged to David Sanborn's sax and David had brought in Carlos Alomar.

Another guitar player, huh?

I didn't know it then, but it turned out he was my replacement.

At the end of the Philly sessions, David said, 'See you in September in LA.'

Then MainMan phoned to break the bad news, 'Slicky, you're not being invited back.'

I was hurt and angry.

Pretty soon, though, David realized he still had a set packed with rock tunes, and Carlos was an R&B player. Before I could make any moves to find a new gig, I got another phone call. MainMan again.

'David got you a ticket to come to LA,' they said.

'Yeah? Why?'

'Oh, you know, you're going to be playing guitar.'

'I am? How much do I get paid?'

They told me how much, and I immediately shot back, 'Nope.'

I may have been young, and an out-of-work guitar slinger, but I told them to go fuck themselves. What a ballsy little fucker I was.

To David's credit, he really did want to be a soul artist at that point in his career. It wasn't like a ploy or a marketing trick or anything like that. He loved the music and he wanted to make that kind of record. That's why we recorded *Young Americans* in Philly. Think about it: Barry White, the Philly Sound and the studio Sigma Sound was where they recorded all that shit. Plus, having someone like Carlos, who had played with people like the O'Jays and James Brown, and the backup singers, some of whom had worked with some serious, old-school R&B bands, made it the real deal.

I'd been fired that summer – between what was the real Diamond Dogs Tour and when David moved on to soul-land – because I think David really believed he was going to go out there and be a soul man, and he didn't need a rock guitar player. And then he woke up one morning and went, 'Holy fuck. What am I going to do for "Suffragette City" and "Cracked Actor"? Who's going to play that shit?' So really he had no choice. It was either Mick Ronson or me, and I don't think there was enough money they could print to get Mick to come back at the time.

Eventually we came to terms. But I needed to stick to my guns to feel like I was coming back on my own terms. They doubled my salary. It still wasn't much, but at least they doubled it. I flew to Los Angeles to get ready for a week of shows at the Universal Amphitheatre.

When I arrived at SIR, the rehearsal studio in LA, it was practically a new band. We had a different rhythm section – obviously Herbie and Tony were gone – and Michael Kamen was gone, too. Sanborn was still there, as was Pablo Rosario on percussion and Mike Garson on piano, plus Geoff MacCormack, David's pal, still on backing vocals. But there was a bunch of new people, too.

Carlos was already there. He'd been instrumental to the Philly sessions, which Sanborn and Garson had played on as well. And he brought in Luther Vandross, who helped arrange all the vocals, plus his wife Robin Clark, Anthony Hinton and Ava Cherry as background singers.

Carlos didn't really do what I did, and I was sure our styles would complement each other, so from my point of view, there were no hard feelings. But when I came back into the fold, he didn't like it. He thought he was going to own the guitar spot. He's a rhythm player and an R&B guy – and a damn good one – not a rock-and-roll player or really a lead player, at least not for that sort of music. Still, I got the cold shoulder and attitude. I'd have whacked him on the head if I didn't think it would get me fired again.

Meanwhile, the elaborate sets were gone. Instead, David would come on stage and we would do the entire Bowie show, which now included a bunch of his new stuff – songs from the unfinished *Young Americans* album – plus his old stuff, reworked in a sort of soul revue style, but without the props. There was no 'Hunger City', no crane lifting David out over the audience, no singing into a telephone, nothing fancy. It was just the band and background singers, with David doing his thing.

Despite the tension between me and Carlos, the shows were killer right through to Christmas. Best of all, I got to know Luther. Because I never slept, he'd call me up at four or five in the morning. 'You up?'

'Of course I'm up.'

'I'm hungry.'

'Luther, it's fucking four in the morning and we're in Detroit.' But I'd go anyway because I loved hanging out with the guy. We fell out of touch afterwards, but when he resurfaced with a hit record, it put the biggest smile on my face. I thought, 'Good. You showed the motherfuckers.' What a great fucking rags-to-riches story he was.

That's also when I noticed David was disengaging. All of a sudden, a separation went up between him and the band. He didn't have fuck-all to do with us from that point on. And he didn't really seem to give a shit what we did, either.

In retrospect, I think it was a combination of things. Some of it was drug-fuelled and some of it was that he was on to his next thing. It seemed like he wanted to get the damn tour over with, so he could go be a soul man. I also think it had a lot to do with David feeling that he was like a piece of meat, getting sucked dry by the bunch at Main-Man. It certainly seemed like we had almost no days off so they could make as much money as possible.

David disengaged via the drugs he was taking. Eventually, he figured out he wasn't making as much money as he could have been. But he didn't know what to do about it. Besides, as much money as he told me he felt was getting ripped off, he was still getting paid. He was still making lots of money.

I'd started drinking like a fish when I was a teenager. I started using cocaine when I was sixteen. David using all that blow when I got there seemed normal. I thought, 'Oh good, he's a normal guy. He's normal like *me*.' But I was also thinking, 'I don't know how long this is going to last.'

Michael Kamen and Herbie Flowers taught me well. Herbie once said, 'We're all disposable, man. And when you're dealing with stars of David's calibre, you can be gone in a flash.'

We wrapped the tour up at the Omni in Atlanta on 1 December.

After the show, we convened for a party in David's enormous suite at the Hyatt, right next door to the Omni. It was a wild scene with the band and crew, not to mention some of the local cuties, celebrating until the wee hours. Obviously, there was blow all over the fucking place.

Then, out of nowhere, a bunch of guys broke down the door, shouting with handguns drawn, threatening us. We didn't know who they were. They weren't in uniform, and they sure didn't act like authorities of any kind. They looked dirty and scruffy, in street clothes no self-respecting person would be caught dead in. Along with everyone else in the room, I found myself face against a wall, with my hands above my head and my legs spread, next to Eric Barrett, our tour manager. Eric had been Jimi Hendrix's guitar tech, so he'd seen some things. We looked at each other and said almost in unison, 'I hope they're fucking cops.'

In the haze of yelling and screaming and shoving, I was terrified and worried about the stash of blow, a 'doggie bag' I'd nicked from the plentiful supply for later, that was stuffed down in my sock.

But they weren't interested in us. Only David. They did a quick frisk of all of us and once they realized David wasn't in the main living room area the rest of us were hanging out in, they started nosing around the suite. Before they found him in the bedroom, he had time to get rid of the mountains of blow he had back there. Or most it, at least.

The guys did turn out to be cops, and soon enough found enough drugs to satisfy themselves that somebody was going to get arrested. Because it wasn't actually on David, his bodyguard Tony took the rap. With all the money and lawyers and such that MainMan had on retainer, Tony was out of jail in a day. David's manager, Tony DeFries, had a way of making things like that disappear, as any good manager back in those days could.

I'm sure the cops were frustrated by the way it went down because in 1974 it sure would have made somebody's career to bust David Bowie in Atlanta, Georgia, on cocaine possession charges. The funniest part of it was once we realized the guys with guns pointed to our heads were cops, we were relieved, and even happy.

Freaked out but free to go, I spent the night in my hotel room trying to dry out the stash in my sock, which was now wet through with nervous sweat. I sat there for what seemed like forever blowing on the coke and waving it over the heater in my room, trying to salvage whatever I could from that crazy experience.

With the tour over, David called me in to help put the finishing touches on *Young Americans* in New York at the Electric Ladyland, the studio built by Jimi Hendrix. Best of all, David brought in a hero of mine to help cut the last two tracks: John Lennon.

John fucking Lennon.

We cut 'Fame' and 'Across the Universe', the old Beatles tune, with John. Unfortunately, I was so out of it that I don't remember much, but I did recognize that David was going for a more commercial version of the sound he'd captured in Philly, and that the album had really started to fall into place.

I love 'Fame' but 'Young Americans' is a bona fide great tune. And clever. I knew it was a hit the first time I heard it. It was the right song at the right time, with a great vocal performance.

But just like Herbie had warned me, it became evident how disposable we all were, given David's career trajectory. He was hanging out with John Lennon and was practically killing himself with drugs. So, I figured I'd just go about my business like I always had.

And so, early in 1975, I got a deal for my own Earl Slick Band with Capitol Records, on the back stairwell of SIR, the rehearsal studio in New York City, with the vice-president of the company, Rupert Perry, and Bob Buziak and Al Coury, who went on to start RSO Records with Bob Stigwood. We were making a record and getting ready to tour when David called.

'Put the band on hold,' he told me. 'Get out to Los Angeles.'

'But I've made this record.'

'Don't worry about that. Get out to Los Angeles.'

Reunited in 2018 with the gold disc I received for playing
on *Station to Station*.

6

The Return of the Thin White Duke

By the time the Diamond Dogs Tour had ended, and the sessions for *Young Americans* were over, things seemed to have changed between me and David and MainMan. The one thing that hadn't changed, regardless of whatever was going on there, was that I was still Earl Slick, now known as David Bowie's guitar player. And that I was using drugs. Heavy.

Then, out of the blue, I got that call.

You'd think I'd be reluctant to work with David again. But I wasn't. By that point, David's erratic behaviour seemed completely normal to me. I didn't think twice about it. The sales of *Young Americans* had been cool, but I'd grown up playing the real thing – real R&B – and it didn't feel authentic. It just didn't. That could be a little bit of sour grapes coming from me, but at the end of the day, *Station to Station* ended up a far superior album in every way, and it helped me even more than getting the Diamond Dogs Tour with David in the first place.

Station to Station is absolutely one of the true highlights of my career. It was an amazing collaborative effort among everyone involved, but most especially between me and David. David pulled shit out of me that I didn't even know was there. He really did. Because all those overdubbed parts were me and David, working together, in the most adventurous and creative ways possible.

We kicked off things in a crummy little rehearsal space in Hollywood. Me, David, Carlos, Dennis Davis on drums and George Murray on bass. This was one shit hot band.

'Stay' started out as a reworked version of David's Ziggy-era tune 'John, I'm Only Dancing'. He asked me to come up with a riff and it turned out to be a total monster, and 'Stay' pretty soon evolved into its own thing.

As for 'Golden Years', David pretty much had it written. He just didn't have a lick at the front end. That was where I came in. Just like 'Stay'. I'm sure David thought while making it that the song could be the single. And it was.

Meanwhile, 'Wild Is the Wind' was a Nina Simone song, so we just learnt it and turned it into a Bowie song.

The rest of the songs were just bits of ideas that David had that we chipped away at together. Even 'TVC 15' was a pretty fully formed idea that David brought to the sessions. What he needed more than anything were signature licks, which I set about creating with relish. That is except for 'Station to Station', the song, because that was a Frankenstein of three of his ideas that got cobbled together as only David could.

Once again, David had changed his working style. He didn't sit us down to let us know his vision for the record. Often when you work with an artist, they'll give you a speech on the first day. 'This is the direction we're going to take this album in.' Like when we came to make *Young Americans*, David made it very clear he wanted to make a soul record. On this one, there wasn't any of that. It was just, 'Okay, we're making a record, this is what I've got.' He played what he had on guitar and then we started playing along and jamming on the stuff in that shitty little rehearsal space until it started to gel. So that was weird and different, but cool, too.

Song by song it started to come together. Once we got into Cherokee Studios, on Fairfax Avenue in Los Angeles, things happened really fast.

Cherokee was a funky place, run by these old folkies, the Robb brothers. *Station to Station* was one of the first mega albums recorded there. The building that housed the studio was an ugly industrial space. Inside, we recorded in non-descript warrens with dark tan walls and brown shag carpet on the floors, while the control room looked like any other recording studio of the time, with black swivel chairs behind a big mixing desk, with loads of outboard gear and huge speakers mounted on the ceiling, and more brown shag carpet on the floor.

The great thing about working with David this time around was that he was now a big star, who had just scored a Number 1 record that featured John Lennon. We were treated like we owned the place. We set up camp like we were going to live there for the next few months, and that's just what we did.

Right away, on the first day, we got to work, fresh off the pre-production work we'd done. We'd jam away on the songs while David would sing the bits of lyrics that he had. As always, just like with any new material I ever cut with David, he didn't have anything 100 per cent finished.

He would hum his way through the verses. But the choruses of the songs were mostly in place. The rough lyrics and decent bassline of the melody he wanted made our jobs pretty easy.

As things fell into place when David heard things he liked, and inspiration hit him, he'd let you know it. He'd say, 'Yup, that's it. That's the one.' And that would be that. If he ever said that, then you knew you were on to something and to focus in on it and keep doing it. That made it really easy, because most of the time in the studio you're playing things pretty randomly, searching for the right feel and part. As soon as he let you know he liked what he was hearing, that was it. Do it again, better, and let's move on.

Soon, I could predict when he'd like something. When he pointed to what he wanted, I almost always agreed. A few times, when I wasn't quite sure, I said, 'Give me another second because I think I can make this a little bit better.' And he'd say, 'Go ahead.' But that was pretty rare. We almost always agreed.

They weren't long days at Cherokee. We did eight to ten-hour stints, and there were only four of them. We'd never recorded with George on bass or Dennis on drums before, but pre-production made a huge difference. Once we got locked in together, we started cutting tracks. It wasn't this discombobulated process that other people have said it was. It was more together than that. I know it's been portrayed as though David came in with a few chords, then we filled in the blanks and *we* put it together, but that's not true. The framework for the songs came together quickly, even though they changed once we started overdubbing.

They were pretty damn close to finished songs, except for the title track, and he worked through them like you would with any band. We'd play them a few times until they started to feel good, and then David would say, 'Okay, that feels like we can start recording them.' In those couple of days, we recorded the skeletons for all of the songs except for the title track, which was still in pieces.

I've got to tip my hat to Dennis Davis and George Murray. Their rhythm section was a motherfucker. Carlos and I, we were fine. We worked off each other well and because our styles are so different, it was self-evident what part each of us would play. That gave the record an open, and special, sound. If you listen closely, there's no doubled rhythm guitars on those tracks. Carlos is on one side, I'm on the other side. For as big as the record sounds, the guitars are really spare.

In fact, the only stacking of guitars that went on was done by me and David, during the overdub sessions. On 'TVC 15', cut live with Roy Bittan on piano, I played all the guitars on that song, except for the chorus part, which was me and David. And if you listen to it, there are a lot of guitars underneath what's up front in the mix, which you'd really notice if you took them away. But on most of the songs, it was just me and Carlos doing our rhythm thing on the left and right, and George and Dennis doing their thing.

Roy was a big part of the sound of the record. David was familiar with Springsteen, because the one thing David did do his whole life was to keep up with what was going on. He knew what Springsteen sounded like, and he knew what his band sounded like. So, when David had asked me before the sessions began if I had ideas for a piano player, and I replied, 'Springsteen's in LA, and his piano player and I have been friends for forever. His name is Roy Bittan,' David said, 'Great. Find him. Get him in here.' Roy had the job before he even knew about it.

Geoff MacCormack was important, too. He was there because David didn't really have any friends around at that time that he could trust. David trusted Geoff. He was also called upon to come up with some backing vocal ideas. Geoffrey was around for a lot of the basic tracks, as well as when we were doing guitar overdubs. He would pop in, just to say hello or whatever, and because David liked to bounce things off him. He had the longest history with David of any of us, so having him around was important, especially given the state David was in, and because there was some business stuff going on there that I'm sure he wouldn't trust anybody but Geoffrey with.

Meanwhile, Harry Maslin was the most easygoing guy you could imagine working with and the perfect producer for that record. Not taking anything away from Harry, but in all the time I spent with David over the years, whether it was putting together live shows or making records, David was really the producer and arranger. It was his concepts; he was the producer. Harry was there to take whatever David was thinking and doing and make sure it ended up on tape and sounded right. That's what Harry's role was. There are some production skills needed in order to do that, because it wasn't just engineering, of course. Harry had to read into what David was talking about to know how to construct his ideas sonically. For instance, most producers, or even just about any mixer or engineer, would have pushed my guitars that are underneath 'Word on a Wing' and 'TVC 15' a lot louder. But Harry knew instinctively where to put them, which was in the background, as an atmospheric thing. He had to think those things through. So, he sure knew what to do.

A lot has been written about the state David was in during the sessions for *Station to Station*. Hell, even David talked a lot about how bad a shape he was in at the time. The reality was that from the first day of rehearsals in Hollywood, I noticed he was visibly worse off than he was when we finished up the '74 run of live dates. He appeared thinner than he'd been, which was pretty fucking thin to begin with. He was wearing a big, oversized fedora and some baggy pants and a T-shirt, which only accentuated it. His behaviour was getting out there, too. Most of all, his cocaine habit was at its peak at that point, and that's saying something, considering the way he'd been inhaling blow on the second leg of the Diamond Dogs Tour. He definitely looked like there was a progression of his drug use that had taken a toll on his body, but it wasn't really like he was on another planet or anything like that. Considering the condition he was in, he was pretty focused.

It wasn't evident that something was seriously off until we started recording. We would work a normal day, and then we'd have the studio booked for the next day, and he'd be a no-show for a couple of days. Zero. Nothing. Eventually, somebody would call the studio and say he wasn't coming in, so we'd jam. Because the studio was already paid for, and there was a chance David could show, we had to stick around. It seemed silly to let the time go to waste. In the end, I brought in the guys from the Earl Slick Band and with Carlos and the rhythm section, we made demos of some of the songs that we'd been working on. The engineer recorded them, not Harry, and we did some pretty cool versions of the songs. Sadly, I have no idea where the tapes ended up.

Once we did get the basic tracks for all the songs down, David and Harry focused their attention on getting the overdubs done. There was more time spent on the overdubs on that album than on any album I've ever worked on, but that's where things got creative. That's where the sessions went into the great unknown. I had no idea what we were going to do with those basic tracks until we got to work on the overdubs, even though the melodies, and even most of the vocals, were in place, or at least close enough to it that we had the vibe that David was going for.

Eventually, it was just me and David doing a lot of overnighters. We were both in a cocaine haze, so it wasn't unusual for him to call at eleven o'clock at night, and that's when we'd start. We'd just keep working until we were done, which could be anywhere from ten to twelve to twenty-four hours later, working straight through.

We would listen to the track he wanted to work on, and David would come up with an idea. He'd say, 'I need this kind of atmosphere here.' Then we'd sit there, both of us with guitars, knocking ideas back and forth. He wasn't as proficient on the guitar, but he was great at expressing what he wanted from you – the vibe – using my hands to get on tape what was in his head.

I was there with him to give him what he thought of as the 'Earl Slick sound' for the overdubs. Because he wanted that. Because he knew that, as much as I was a pretty staunch, old-school rock-and-roll and blues player, I was also capable of comprehending when he wanted to go off the beaten path and that I understood what he was talking about. When he wanted something that was on the out-side, he knew he could get that out of me. Because I trusted him when he had these seemingly left-field ideas that they were going to fit, I just went for it, and it always seemed to work.

Sometimes, he would play the bit as best as he could, and then I would play it. Because I was a more competent guitarist, I often nailed it right away. He'd go, 'I want this sound on this rhythm bit on "TVC 15".' And then he'd show me the way he wanted it done. On that one, both of us played that chorus, with those fat-sounding guitars playing together at the same time. And then underneath he had me layer all sorts of little parts. If you listen to that song closely, there's a lot going on. But it doesn't appear that way. How he mixed it, you don't hear those nuances right away. It's like looking at a van Gogh painting. You see 'The Starry Night' and you see the big picture. But the more you look at it, the more you go, 'Holy shit. Look at that bit. And look at this bit over there.'

Other times, though, David would give me just the roughest morsel of an idea to go on. Barely anything. And then he'd let me go to town.

Or he'd say, 'Okay, Slicky, what do you need to do on this section here?' I'd reply, 'I'm not sure yet. Throw something at me.' And we would sit there, sometimes for hours, just messing around. I might try a hundred different ideas and, all of a sudden, David would just up and say, 'Yup, you got it. That's it right there.' And then we would home in on how I was playing what he liked until it fitted sonically.

That's why that record is special and has lasted so long. It was a true collaboration. Not just between me and David, of course, but Harry and Carlos and Dennis and George and Roy, as well.

The song 'Station to Station' was a whole other animal, unlike anything we'd ever done together, and actually unlike anything that had been attempted in rock and roll before.

As for the groaning guitars in the intro, they just came out of nowhere. The tracks were already cut when David said, 'We need something at the beginning of this.' The next thing I know, somebody made a phone call, and half a dozen 100-watt stacks of Marshalls rolled into the studio. Harry and his crew lined them up along the back wall, all mic'ed up, and me and David plugged in and we're playing at top volume, just feeding back.

We switched back and forth, because I remember doing some of it on a Fender Strat and some of it on a Gibson Les Paul. But we were in the room, together, playing eyeball to eyeball at the same time. It was fun as hell, man. Because who else would do this? Who else *could*? Here I am, six o'clock in the morning, coked out of my brain, feeding back like a maniac. I didn't know what the hell it had to do with music, but it was a riot.

In order to attack it, we broke it down into sections. We

had names for the sections. Once we had the basic track recorded, and we set about overdubbing the guitars, David used those sections to direct me. For the opening, he said, 'Keith Richards, Chuck Berry.' On the second section, he said, 'Remember that bit you did on "Sweet Thing" with Davie? I want that lick.' Immediately, I remembered this little lick I played that I'd gotten from David Sanborn. It was a weird, dissonant thing that I used on *David Live*. If you listen to the solo, you'll hear it.

Because we mapped it out, and did it piece by piece, we spent more time on that solo than I've ever done on any record in my life. That was me and David with Harry Maslin and David Heinz, who was what they called at the time a 'tape op', but who was really the second engineer. That was it. It was just us in there. And the results were magical.

Nobody really thinks of David as a guitar player, but he was more than capable of getting across what he wanted if he was in the mood to do it. One thing he had that lots of guys don't was sonics. He could hear things on a level most people couldn't understand. If you have *Diamond Dogs* and listen to the guitar solo on 'Sweet Thing', that's David. There's no way in hell a guitar player that was just a guitar player would ever do something like that. Between the notes he was playing and the sound he was creating, guitar players don't think like that. So, his guitar playing was definitely the shit. And that's where I learnt a lot from David, about texture and coming at things from a song-writer's point of view.

Maybe I didn't have a picture in my head of what I was going to do, but I knew that whatever it was, it was something that David could hear in his head. I knew that much. I quickly learnt what it was that he heard. While it wasn't mapped out in a traditional sense because ideas would just come to him, out of the blue, on the spot, it was my job to be able to give it back to him, right there and then, before the inspiration evaporated. But he'd also stay with you until it was done, which is very unusual on any of the records I've done.

Even though the drug use spun out of control during making *Station*, it didn't affect David's creativity or my playing. If anything, it affected what I played in a good way because when you're up long enough – like for two fucking days – your inhibitions go. Your brain goes. And you'll do things that you wouldn't normally think of doing, either because you can't think anymore and you're operating on some other level or because it's your unconscious operating. In fact, with that many drugs in your system, you're unconscious, even though you're walking around.

Looking back, we were so high all the time I'm not sure how that record ever got finished, or how he could even sing because we'd be on a roll in the studio for days at a time, never stopping. But David's vocals on the album are all amazing, and he did those in the midst of all that insanity.

It wasn't as though we said to ourselves, 'Hey, you know how we can make a really cool and supremely weird record? Let's do too much cocaine, stay up for days at a time until we're completely sleep-deprived, until we don't have any inhibitions left. Let's make a record like that.' It wasn't like that. Nevertheless, in all honesty, if there was no cocaine, there would be no *Station to Station*. Not the way it turned out, at least. It's definitely one of those cases of, 'Don't try this at home, kids.' Because when you stay up that long, and you're that strung out, which we both were, you don't think of things in terms of time, and you certainly don't think of things in terms of the commercial value of the recording. You just do what you do. You lock yourself in the studio and go into the zone. And you're there recording and coming up with ideas. We were just so homed in on what we were doing. Once we walked through that studio door, the entire outside world vaporized. It's very hard to describe it because being there at the time, none of this crossed my mind. It was only years later that I realized that's what was going on.

There are textures on that record. Maybe a couple of songs fall into 'Son of "Fame"' territory, but 'Wild Is the Wind', 'Word on a Wing' and 'Station to Station' are miles apart, and light-years apart sonically. It's interesting, because I'm more capable as a human being and guitarist doing all those disparate styles than I am following directions and maps. Put me in a place where I don't know where I am, and I don't know if the sun's up or down, or where east or west are. Similarly, give me the structure you want for your song – a map – and the results aren't going to be interesting. But ask me to create something from nothing and I'm in my element. David knew he was going to get much better results out of me if he dropped me out of the sky into the middle of nowhere. That's exactly what, in hindsight, was going on. There was no map. He didn't have one. It was a matter of making it up as we went along. And that's probably one of the reasons for the effect

Station to Station had on my career, and the effect it had on the record business, more generally. That was one of the first albums of its kind to ever be made. Looking back on it, the way we worked is probably the part I cherish about it more than anything else.

You've got to remember, Fleetwood Mac were making *Rumours* at the time. McCartney was recording *Wings at the Speed of Sound*. Those albums sounded nothing like *Station to Station*. It's very hard to think of any major artist, somebody of David's stature, going out on a limb in this Krautrock-soul hybrid. In terms of what else was going on at the time, it seems like career suicide. And yet, it's probably his best record, and his most fully realized record. That's not just because I worked on it, but because it was such a groundbreaker. That wasn't our intent. And that's the key. People always try to read something into David's lyrics, or into the sound of the album. Listeners, other musicians, record company people, reviewers have this preconceived idea that we had a preconceived idea. But there wasn't one. It was just a blind journey. We were jumping without a net. It didn't occur to us that that's what we were doing. It was such an odd experience, in hindsight, but normal at the time. We didn't give a thought to what we were doing, which is a hard thing for people to comprehend. And that's really the beauty of *Station to Station*, to me. It was the experience and the journey of making that record that stays with me.

For the record, there was not one word about Krautrock or occultism or any of the other shit people have written about. We were making a rock-and-roll record, and David was simply pushing that medium as far as he could, in the styles he was digging at the moment. But David was clearly in a very dark place. He didn't talk about any of it, but sometimes we would get a call at the last minute that he'd be working on music for the *Man Who Fell to Earth* movie, because he was working on both projects at the same time, or sometimes he just wasn't showing up. But it didn't faze me. Number one, David could afford to do what he wanted, how he wanted, and when he wanted. In other words, if he was incapable of – or simply didn't feel like – coming into the studio, the actual money that was paid for that day was of no consequence to him. He couldn't give a shit. Also, you've got to remember how old he was at the time. David wasn't even thirty. At that age, your body can handle a lot. As far as getting no sleep, doing a lot of drugs and drinking a lot, that was just the way things were in 1975. We didn't know what we know today about those things, especially cocaine. So, everything at least *seemed* normal.

Before I left, David and I talked about going out on tour in 1976 to support the album. But I had already signed with Capitol, and I had a band waiting for me. I said, 'David, what am I going to do about getting my record finished and taking my own band out?' He told me, 'You'll have time to work on the record. Come out with me, and I'll make sure that the guys will get at least a little something every month kicked to them from my end to keep them going while you're gone.' We agreed on that, and I told the band. They weren't thrilled, but at least they knew that they were going to be getting some support money every month.

So that was the plan. We'd talked it through. We didn't

involve management or anything. It was a decision that was made between David and me.

I headed to New York for the holidays at the end of 1975. Rehearsals were supposed to start in Kingston, Jamaica, after the New Year. And that's when shit started to get weird. David and Michael Lippman, who was managing us both at that time, split up. But I was still with Michael, so I became the kid in the middle of the divorce. Mom was pulling one arm, and Dad was pulling the other arm. I had gotten my Capitol deal on my own, but Lippman was the one who had negotiated the fine points. I'd even been staying at his house on and off while I was in LA making *Station*.

I was between a rock and a hard place. Plus, there was one guy left over from MainMan, Pat Gibbons, who I just never got along with, that David had kept on. His role at MainMan was accounting, but after things went south between David and Lippman, Gibbons became David's manager and spokesperson.

I was getting ready to head to Jamaica because I'd gotten a plane ticket in the mail. However, I didn't know what my salary was and I was calling and trying to get through to David to get some more details. Gibbons kept telling me that David wasn't talking to anybody. I said, 'Well, I at least need to know what I'm getting paid.' He told me what they were thinking and I said, 'That's not good enough. I've got to hear this from David.'

That went on for a few weeks.

Finally, I told Gibbons, 'Look, if David doesn't get on that phone, we're going to have a problem.' David never did get on the phone, and so I got on a plane and flew back to LA, instead of Jamaica. I didn't quit. I just didn't show up. I'd become a casualty of David's fallout with his management company, and I was off the tour and back playing bars.

But all was not lost. I hooked up with Jean Millington, the bass player in Fanny, the groundbreaking, all-female group. We were a twenty-five-year-old 'It' couple and having the time of our lives. We got married a year later. A daughter and son, Marita and Lee, followed.

It seemed I was done with David. Or so I thought.

An ad for the first Earl Slick Band album. Nuff said . . .

7

Razor Sharp

I started the first Earl Slick Band album in 1975, in the midst of the *Station to Station* sessions. We had the deal with Capitol. We had Harry Maslin producing.

By the time the sessions were wrapping up, in 1976, I figured I was done with David. I'd screwed things up too badly. Or at least I thought.

One afternoon, I was lying on the couch in the studio, when the phone rang.

'Slicky?'

'David?'

'Slicky, I need you back in the band. I'll send a car to pick you up. Just pack a bag. I need you here.'

My fucking head exploded.

David was in town to play the Forum. With his new guitarist, obviously. He gave me a number to call him back on, but I didn't know what the fuck to do. Walk out on the guys in the band, the record deal? Get back on board with David?

In the end, I took the path of least resistance. I didn't call David back. Didn't show up at the Forum. And by the time I realized the mistake I'd made, the hole was too deep to climb out of.

As any Bowie fan will tell you – and certainly any guitar slinger will tell you – this was a monumentally bad decision. Not only did I miss out on the rest of the *Station* tour, but I also potentially missed out on *Low* and *Heroes* and *Lodger*. And, of course, *Scary Monsters*.

That's hindsight, of course. I felt honour bound and committed to my band, the record company and my management because, I guess, things seemed so far along. Even at the time, I had knots in my stomach for a long time. It was a rough one to live with. But I'd made the decision and had to live with it, no matter how much it gnawed at me. And it really did. It ate me up for a good long while.

The band finished up the record and hit the road, so that got me out of my head. By the time we'd finished the tour and doing promo, things had turned around. Everything was cool. I was busy.

Pretty soon, the record company sent me over to England because there was a lot of interest. The record sold a fair amount and Capitol wanted another album. In England we worked with producer John Alcock, who had done the Thin Lizzy *Jailbreak* album, which I really loved. I was a Thin Lizzy fan. Some of the dates we did supporting the first Earl Slick Band record had been opening up for Lizzy a number of times, and I had got to know Phil Lynott and the guys and we became friends. Onstage they were just amazing. Phil would have gone on to do great things. He's one whose best days were ahead of him when he died, and he's sorely missed.

John spent some time with us and he liked the band, so we did a little bit of pre-production, and he booked us in at Ramport Studios, in the Battersea section of London, which was owned by The Who at the time.

So not only did we have the same producer and engineer, we used the same studio that *Jailbreak* had been recorded in. We hunkered down, and we put together the *Razor Sharp* album. If you listen to both of those records, you can see the thread there. You can hear it.

Even though Harry Maslin produced the first album, *Razor Sharp* is a better record, which is unusual. Often a band's first record is their best. But the way I see it, before we did the first album, we had played around a lot as a band, even before I got the job with David, but then I'd disappeared into David's world. When we did the first album, we hadn't been playing those songs live or anything. When we did *Razor Sharp*, though, we came right from doing gigs into the studio. It was fresh. In fact, I was still finishing off the songs in London at a rented house we had while we made the album. I wrote 'Razor Sharp', the title track, during those days in England. It was one of the last songs we recorded on the album.

Plus, John Alcock's approach was harder edged and British, and he was more hands-on than Harry, and that's where my head was at the time. No disrespect at all to Harry, but John really took control, and he really knew what to do with us.

The lead singer was Jimmie Mack. He and I had been working together off and on since we were seventeen years old. We'd had Mack Truck together, and different versions of that band, where Jimmy sang, played rhythm, and some lead guitar. He also wrote most of the songs on his own back then because at the time, I really wasn't a songwriter. The bass player, Gene Leppik, was another guy from Staten Island and Bryan Madey was the drummer. I'd met Bryan when I was managed by MainMan and worked with Dana Gillespie – a hysterical, buxom Brit, who did a lot of old-school double entendre, dirty-mouth blues – and he was the drummer.

The cover of the second album, meanwhile, was a fight to the death with the record company. We wanted a Mylar cover that was raised and embossed – and expensive. It was a stupid fight because they'd already spent a fortune on these little razor blade necklaces that said '*Razor Sharp*, Earl Slick Band' on them. Our promotion guy, Billy Bass, went to bat for me and we got our covers.

After the second album came out, we hit the road again, supporting bands like Kansas and Ted Nugent and, in between, after doing a week of that, we'd have a week on our own, headlining clubs and theatres to about 2,500 people.

Eventually, we started having problems inside the Slick Band. I felt we were starting to fall into that 'club band' mentality, just grinding it out. I wanted to experiment because things felt repetitious. We needed to expand our horizons, but I could not get everybody on the same page. When we tried to write new stuff, I realized Jimmy tended towards one kind of song. I got fed up with things and called it a day.

It was the end of 1976, and another chapter was coming to a close.

Pretty soon, I heard rumblings that Mick Ronson, who

had been in Mott the Hoople after leaving David, and then had worked with Ian Hunter, the lead singer from that band, when he went solo, wasn't working with Ian anymore. One thing led to another and, pretty soon, I ended up on the phone with Ian and then on a plane from LA to New York.

I was quite familiar with Ian's music because I was a Mott fan, as well as a fan of Ronson. Ian and I got along famously. We spent time at his house in upstate New York, jamming and fooling around with some of the new songs he had. After that, we flew over to England and put together the *Overnight Angels* in London at the end of that year. That band was a fucking riot.

We had a drummer from Birmingham named Mac Poole, whose John Bonham-esque drumming was really loud and heavy handed, but solid and with a great groove. We rehearsed with him and a great bass player named Rob Rawlinson, from the British blues band Chicken Shack, and the keyboard player was from Gary Glitter's band, named Peter Oxendale, who was a complete fucking lunatic.

At first it seemed like it was working, but something felt not quite right. Ian already had Roy Thomas Baker on board as producer to make the album, so the clock was ticking. We put our heads together and realized it was Mac who wasn't working. Ian called Dennis Elliot, the drummer on his first solo record, who at the time was playing with Foreigner, but he told Ian that, as much as he loved him, he had made a commitment to Foreigner. But Dennis agreed to do the recording sessions, so we were thrilled. Even though he was on the album, an old friend of mine named Curly Smith, who was in a band called JoJo Gunne with some of the guys from the band Spirit, eventually came in as the permanent drummer. Even though Curly's face appears on the album, it's Dennis playing drums, except for on 'England Rocks', which we recorded with Bill Price at the same Wessex studio where the Sex Pistols recorded *Never Mind the Bollocks*.

That song has had an interesting life. It started off as 'Cleveland Rocks', then it became 'England Rocks' when we recorded it, to capitalize on Ian's popularity in England. Eventually, Ian went back to 'Cleveland Rocks'.

I played the 'Wild N' Free' solo with a splint on my finger because it got cut open and stitched up the day before when I put my hand through a window. I showed up at the studio the next day, when we were set to record the solo to 'Wild N' Free'. Stitches or not, I did what was needed.

I remember thinking that I'd really hit one out of the park with Ian. Ian was red hot at the time, Roy Baker was on fire and I was on fire, too.

Once the record was finished, we prepared to go out live, rehearsing in Dobbs Ferry, New York, in a loft space in one of those old late-1800s two-storey buildings above some businesses. We would rehearse at night, obviously, because once the stores closed down, we could make all the noise we wanted to.

One day I got a call from one of the guys. 'There's no rehearsal today.' I asked him what was going on and he said, 'We had a little problem. The gear got stolen.'

Cops on foot patrol noticed that the door of the rehearsal space was open in the middle of the night. They went and checked on it to discover they were too late. The crew that had been there left in a rush and didn't shut the doors properly. Thieves had cleaned us out.

The heist turned out to have been masterminded by a guy working for us. Okay, he also happened to be my blow dealer at the time. On that winter night, he showed up with a truck, loaded it up and disappeared. We never found him.

Pretty soon we headed for England, and then Europe, for a long tour. While we were on the road, Ian's manager apparently caused a real uproar at Columbia Records, and we got some rumblings while touring England and Europe that things in the States were going awry. I don't really know what he did, but whatever happened, they decided not to release the album in the US.

A couple of weeks later, Ian sat me down. 'We're kind of fucked,' he said, looking and sounding dejected and more than a little angry. The label had cut off funding, so there was no more retainer. I was fucking shattered.

You've got to be fucking kidding me. I finally get in with a band that I have a piece of – because Ian insisted on it being an actual band – with a little bit of the songwriting money, and I'm on the cover, and then something goes down between the manager and the label and it scuttles the whole thing. Times like this one make you realize you're not the one flying the plane.

That was the end of that. The retainer had been cut off. We had nothing to live on. I'd put everything on hold for that project, moving back to New York to work with Ian, and I had rent to pay, but I had no money. I know Ian was justified to be pissed when everyone scattered. It was just the situation, though. We had two Brits and two guys from the West Coast – me and the drummer Curly Smith. Once the funding was gone, we were all stuck in upstate New York with no way to survive because we were in the band full time. We had our backs against the wall. So off I went, back to Los Angeles. That was the beginning of a tough period.

I floundered around, trying to find the right thing to get involved with. I lived in the Hollywood Hills – back then you could get an inexpensive apartment in a pretty decent area – but things were tough. I'd gotten married at the end of 1976, so when I got back, I figured I'd better start calling everyone under the sun and find some work, pronto. Even though there was no more Mott the Hoople, Ian was on the radar. He was rocking. People had the misconception that I was unavailable. I had to get out and let everybody know that I was a gun for hire. I did demo sessions and weird little gigs here and there. What came out of that period was interesting because I ended up working with Tonio K – the 'Amazing Mr K' as I used to call him – on his signature *Life in the Foodchain* album, which the great Rob Fraboni produced.

The album slipped through the cracks at the time because it was just too weird and progressive. I did most of the demos, and when it came time to do the record proper, I did the whole thing, which was a real trip. At first, I couldn't make heads or tails of Tonio because he was like a punk-pop-rock version of Bob Dylan. While what he was doing was strange, I really liked it. And I liked him. We made what is now considered one of those 'cult' records that, over the years, people became aware of and embraced. Now it's considered iconic, especially for the time it was made. Most people aren't familiar with the album, but there are amazing songs on there. And the lyrics are next level.

Politics tinged Tonio's lyrics and he was tongue-in-cheek, as well. A song or two concerned his ex-wife in there, but the way he wrote wasn't an 'I'm going to cry in my beer at the bar, my wife just left me' kind of thing. The songs were subversive and deeper than they appeared. 'How Come I Can't See You in My Mirror?' featured me and Albert Lee on guitars together. At first listen you wonder if maybe the song is about a vampire. But it isn't. It was about someone he knew and missed. The political songs were very cleverly put-together, lyrically. On a song called 'H-A-T-R-E-D' on the album, you can hear this organ coming, and then Roger Nichols, who'd showed up with an AK-47, proceeds to unload. You hear actual gun-shots on the record. That's how the song ends. Some of the bullets during the recording of the song ricocheted into people's homes nearby. The next thing we knew, there were police everywhere.

If you have the desire to find the album and give it a listen, I recommend you do. The more you hear it, the more you appreciate it. It's a gem that just got lost. Tonio went on to become a successful songwriter, writing a lot of Charlie Sexton's early music.

It was a true learning experience for me but, as with most growth moments, I didn't know that I was learning anything until after the fact. Later, it hit me. Holy shit, there was a lot more going on than I realized while it was happening. Coming from David and Ian, I'd felt like I'd taken a big step backward. Most of the stuff I was doing was to feed the bank account and I took anything and everything I could get my hands on.

Frustrated, I became hellbent on putting a band together. I wanted to do my own thing and I'm a bull in a china closet when I set my mind to something. That's where my band Silver Condor came in.

Of course, it was all about finding the right lead singer and the right team. A friend of mine from New York suggested a singer named Joe Cerisano, who at the time was living in New Jersey. He flew out, and damn he could sing. He was a really good pop writer, too.

We had good management because I was signed with Premier Talent Agency. Barbara Skydel, who was my personal agent at Premier, the biggest agency on the planet at that point, worked right under Frank Barsalona, the legendary agent. She put us together with Bruce Lundvall, who was running Columbia Records at the time. Barbara was right in there with the right people and really took care of me. Barbara, who's sadly no longer with us, was as much of a great friend as she was a great agent. For twenty years of my life she looked after me. She was an angel and the big sister I'd never had.

We had a deal in five minutes. And it was not a small deal. Getting a record deal meant that I'd got a band, I'd got a vehicle and I could make money. My plan for Silver Condor was for it to have a hard blues style, but Joe took it in a pop direction.

We ended up with a Top 40 single, written by the

keyboard player, John Corey. It was high enough in the charts that we were doing shows like *Solid Gold* and *Merv Griffin*. We toured the States. We did a lot of gigs opening up for Peter Frampton, who was, of course, red hot at the time, playing 20,000-seat halls.

In the middle of all this, without any warning, the phone rang again. It was a call that would change my life in ways I could not possibly have imagined.

In the studio with John, Yoko and my wife, Jean.
Our daughter Marita is on John's knee.

8

There's Only One John & Yoko

In the late spring of 1980, my manager, Trudy Green, got a call from the producer Jack Douglas. Jack is a stand-up guy, and an amazing producer. His multi-platinum work with Aerosmith and Cheap Trick alone means he's alright in my book.

Of course, it was another one of those mysterious situations that I'd gotten used to. But first off, Trudy got the call and she jumped into action. She got on the phone with Columbia and got them to push Silver Condor's recording dates back. Then she got me on the phone, pronto, with Jack. Jack tried to play cat-and-mouse and the ole 'I'm not gonna tell you who it is' game. But I did the math. I knew it was John Lennon.

See, I don't take anything anybody says and just leave it there. I'm a sceptic, always doubting what people tell me and investigating things for myself. I need to look at what the fuck's going on. My number one thing is to be prepared. I don't like surprises. It's one thing to be surprised when it's a new artist, but it's a whole other ballgame when it's David Bowie or John Lennon.

The first thing I deduced was that if Jack Douglas was telling me he's got something going on, it wasn't an audition. It was an actual job. When he wouldn't tell me who the session was with, I started thinking. I knew Jack and his history. I knew what he'd been doing lately, as well as who he'd worked with in the past. He sure wasn't calling me for a Cheap Trick session. Or to play with Aerosmith, for that matter, because I'd have heard about that. That would've been news if somebody in Aerosmith had quit, right? So, I eliminated both bands he'd worked with recently. Then I went back and thought, 'Wait a minute, who's Jack worked with that's so big that he can't or won't tell me who it is on a phone call booking me for a record? Who's been missing for a little while? Who haven't we heard from?'

I called Trudy and I told her, 'When Jack calls up next time, just say the words "John Lennon" and see how he reacts.'

Later that day she called back. 'Silence.' That was her answer. And she said Jack got anxious when she said John's name and told her to 'keep it quiet.' Well, that was too easy. Of course I'd keep things quiet. But there's no doubting I was really excited because here I am now at a point where, over my time in the business, I'd ended up being involved with most of the people that had been instrumental in me picking up the guitar. I'd been a Dr. John fan before I'd ever met and worked with him. David? You bet! Ian Hunter? Same thing. I always went for the controversial, rebellious fuckers. The complete anarchists. The guys who don't give a shit. I always love those artists because not giving a shit is what keeps me alive.

So here I am, and here's The Beatle who didn't give a

shit. John Lennon did what he did, said what he said, and that was that. I always loved that about him. With the opportunity to work with him, I felt as though, of all the Beatles, this was the right Beatle for me.

Now, I never get nervous. Ever. I'd been in a room with all kinds of people up to that point. But that first day working with John, I got nervous. This was a real 'holy shit' moment. Some of the guys who had been hired to work on what would become *Double Fantasy* – John's comeback album after taking five years off to raise his son Sean – had gotten cassettes of John's demos, and had been up to the Dakota, the Upper West Side Gothic building where he and Yoko lived, to run through things. But not me. I basically got a plane ticket and a hotel reservation and a day and time that I was supposed to show up at a studio. Beyond that, I got no plan. Nothing. As prepared as I like to be, I had no clue what the hell was going on, or what would be expected of me.

There was a reason for that. John and Jack, I found out later, wanted to bring me in cold. I wasn't going to be reading charts. Jack knew I couldn't, anyway. And I wasn't going to be playing stock stuff – pre-arranged parts – because Jack knew I wouldn't. That was for Hugh McCracken to do.

Hugh was a fantastic guy, and a really great guitar player. He'd played sessions with everybody, including Paul McCartney. And the parts he came up with for John were amazing and perfect. Huey's parts are all the cool shit on that record. Huey taught me a lot, too, in those sessions. I watched Huey. He was a really good teacher.

95

But that wasn't my job. I was the wildcard.

On 6 August, the first day of the sessions at the Hit Factory in New York City, I was the first guy there. Or at least I thought I was. John beat me to the studio. Hours before we were supposed to be there, he arrived alone, just hanging out in the big, empty studio. In retrospect, I think he was a little apprehensive. He didn't really know anybody, and this was his big 'comeback'. Even when you're John Lennon, or maybe especially when you're John Lennon, that's a lot of pressure.

The biggest thing that had to be weighing on John was that he hadn't made a record in five years, which in 1980 was a helluva long time. He was anxious, I'm sure. Not about me, or about any of the guys, really. About the *whole thing*. I mean, what the hell? Five years? From thirty-five years of age to forty years of age? That's a huge disappearing act. If you're Joe Blow, you're dead. You're out the ball game. But if you're a Beatle, you can disappear for five years. But it still doesn't mean you just waltz back onto the scene. No way.

It really was like starting over, as John would say on the first single from the record. Up to that point, he had made all his solo records with a core group of guys: Ringo, Klaus Voormann, Jim Keltner, Billy Preston, Jesse Ed Davis. But this was going to be a situation where he would be working with all new people because John wanted new blood and a new outlook. That meant that he needed to surround himself with a new team, other than Jack, that is, because he wanted to have at least one person he knew from the old days that he could rely on to bounce ideas off, which was totally understandable. And not just musical ideas, mind you, but things like, 'Is this the right band? Am I going in the right direction?' John trusted Jack with that.

I walked into the studio that day early because I was nervous about everything. I told myself, okay, I'll get there, I'll calm down, I'll chill out. I'll noodle on my guitar. I'll get my shit together before John shows up. My gear had shipped to the studio, so I knew I had everything I needed there already, but when I got off the elevator on the sixth floor of the Hit Factory, there wasn't any A or B studio. Instead there was just one big room on the sixth floor – and who was sitting in the middle of the room, but John Fucking Lennon.

There was no gear in there yet. The room was completely empty save a chair in the middle of this room, with John sitting on it, playing his guitar.

I thought, 'Oh, so much for getting here early.'

John looked really cool. He was tanned and his hair was really long, like on the cover of The Beatles' *Abbey Road* album. He wore a black cowboy shirt with smiley pockets on it, and jeans with boots. He was slighter and taller than I expected. Lanky.

I went over and introduced myself. We had a good start because we both played on David's *Young Americans* album. John had written 'Fame' with David, and I had played on that. I had also played on 'Across the Universe', the cover of The Beatles' song David cut for that album. At least I think that was me. I'm credited.

And John said I was there.

In fact, I didn't remember John and me being in the studio at the same time, but when I walked in that day, and

I walked over to John and said, 'Good to meet you,' John laughed and said, 'Good to see you again.'

Huh? He insisted we had met during the *Young Americans* sessions, but I didn't remember any of it. I took his word for it, though, because he seemed sure and I was pretty out of it in 1975, so anything was possible. I mean, my fingers were working just fine, because the record sounds okay, but who knows where my brain was at.

But how could I forget meeting John Lennon?

That became a running joke, from that first day right through the whole recording process. And I think it created a bit of a bond because here's this guy who had influenced the entire planet, and I couldn't remember that I'd met him before. Well, John thought that was pretty great shit because it made him a human being instead of this deity to be worshipped, and that's a big deal for a guy like that. I think he found it refreshing that I had the balls to say I didn't remember him. I could've played along, though it's not in my nature to do that. 'Nope, I don't remember you.' It was funny as shit to John, and every once in a while during the sessions, we'd be in the middle of a take and he'd turn to me, look over his glasses, and say, 'You remember me now?'

With the ice broken, we started talking. And from pretty much that moment on, it was like hanging out with any other musician. We were just a couple of guys having a cup of coffee and some cigarettes. It was cool. I got over my nervousness pretty quickly. As soon as the initial, 'Wow, there's John Lennon,' passed, and we had talked for five minutes, that was it. Gone.

Right away, I noticed he had this great New York vibe. Strangely, our backgrounds were pretty similar. Maybe the way we grew up was different because of situations at home and stuff, but we both grew up in pretty grungy, working-class areas as kids. At the time I didn't think about that, but that shared sensibility had a lot to do with why we hit it off. We really came from similar places as kids. And I think that's why the relationship we formed in those first few minutes hanging out in the live room of the Hit Factory stayed tight, through the whole process of recording, and even afterwards.

I still didn't even know what we were doing when I got there that first day. I didn't know what kind of record John was making, or really if he was even making a record. And I certainly didn't know we were going to be making two albums at once, which was how it turned out. We made what would become *Double Fantasy* and *Milk and Honey*, which came out after John was killed, at the same time.

I also didn't know if we were making a Yoko Ono record or a John Lennon record because we were recording songs by both of them, and that eventually the songs were going to be intermingled with each other. People always refer to those albums as John's albums. They're not. Half of those records are Yoko's material. Only half of it is John's brainchild. It's a dialogue that goes back and forth. It's a double fantasy. Literally. Do the math. Look at the lyrics. They're yelling at each other, and they're making love with each other, and they're ignoring each other. Listen now to the songs and there's a flow to them. It's a conversation. It was an idea that was way ahead of its time. And if you listen to the records like that, as a conversation between two people who have been through a whole shitload of stuff that nobody else on the planet would have even dreamed of going through – a Beatle being adored and idolized by an entire culture of people, and then that band breaking up, and this mysterious Japanese woman who everyone blames the breakup on, who had nothing to do with the fucking thing – and here we are all these years later, nearly twenty years after the *Ed Sullivan Show*, as husband and wife, partners and co-artists.

I remember watching them making that record together and I thought it was the coolest thing. But, at the time, the public was not in favour of it. They wanted a John Lennon comeback album, sure. But a John and Yoko album? No way. Yoko was still being looked at as the devil, which was such bullshit as far as I was concerned. The public always looks for a scapegoat, so after the Beatles broke up, who were they going to blame? There were women involved? And a foreigner to boot? Forget it.

I found that somewhere between disgusting and ridiculous. The ridiculous part was that the fans didn't know anything about their relationship. They were making a judgment without knowing anything about John and Yoko. The disgusting part was that they were literally judging the book by its cover. Period. And it was their version of what the cover looked like, which was highly inaccurate. This was John and Yoko's lives we're talking about. Yoko was an easy scapegoat.

Maybe that was why I loved her, right from the first minute of meeting her. But it was also because, in short order, I realized that I was dealing with another strong personality. Damn, she was tough. Tiny and elegant, but a force of nature, too. And cool as shit. That was evident right away. I remember thinking, these people are the real deal. And so we went ahead, recording one of John's songs and one of Yoko's songs.

Pretty soon the rest of the band showed up. Hugh McCracken, of course, was the other guitarist, Tony Levin played bass, George Small was on keyboards, Tony Davilio handled the musical arrangements and horn parts, Andy Newmark was the drummer and Arthur Jenkins added percussion.

We started with one of John's tunes on that first day, but we didn't go through a set list of the songs he had for the album. We'd do a couple at a time, just banging them around until they started to come together, becoming a band in the process. Once we got rolling and into a routine, Lee DeCarlo, the engineer, would be there before everybody arrived, doing clean up or whatever, making sure everything was ready to go. Jack would show up later, which was really not a major issue because John had so much experience in the studio. Plus, Lee was a helluva engineer. And Yoko knew what she was doing, too. So, it was fine.

The vibe was cool, whether Jack or John was running the session, or Yoko was in charge. The band would come in and after everybody set up, we would hang out for maybe an hour, and we'd listen to a demo John or Yoko had made of whatever song they wanted to tackle. The other guys already had their charts, so they'd tell me what key it was in. If I got stumped, I'd look at Huey. I'd say,

'What the hell was that chord? Oh, it's one of these. Okay, great.' I didn't know what to call them. Huey would say, 'That's a demented chord.' Or a diminished, or whatever the fuck it was. I'd learn all of the little nuances and off we'd go.

John would get in the vocal booth with his guitar and he would sing and play live. He wanted that live feel. On a lot of the final takes that were chosen as the masters, part of that vocal, if not the majority, were the live vocals John cut with him just patching things up here and there.

John's rhythm guitar, as well, came almost completely from what he cut live, playing with the band. That was essential to the way the songs turned out, especially on the rockier tunes, because John, unbeknownst even to me, was one hell of a rhythm guitar player. I'd always liked the way he'd played, having seen him all those times on TV and in films with The Beatles. But you can't really judge what kind of player a guy is from that. When I got in the room with the guy, and he was playing, I suddenly realized, 'God! This guy. This rhythm. He's intense. He's beating the shit out of that guitar.'

In fact, John's rhythm wasn't all that far off from the way Keith Richards would treat his guitar, which wasn't a surprise since they drew from the same source: Chuck Berry. Something about the energy, and the rawness of it, and the way he was bashing the guitar made it driving and punky and right up my alley.

Lots of people over the years have asked me about John's Sardonyx guitar, which he used on the sessions, and I've gotta say, it wasn't bad. It looked bizarre, but it played well. It had little switches – coil tap switches – on it, but otherwise there wasn't much to it because it was just one straight plank with these weird pontoons hanging off it, which were made of, I think, hollowed-out aluminium. I don't know why they were there, but there was nothing to them. The guitar was oh so light.

I had discussions with John about guitars a few times, but when he broke that one out, I said, 'What the fuck is that thing you're playing?' In the end, I bought one, too! I ended up selling it, but it wasn't a bad guitar.

One day I asked him what happened to The Beatles, guitars from the *Ed Sullivan* period and his early days. A few days later, he brought them in for me to check out. The short-necked Rickenbacker was busted – it had been broken since the sixties, he said.

And the third guitar story I have about John is that I used my J-45 on all of the acoustic tracks I did on *Double Fantasy* except one song, on 'Beautiful Boy', when John brought me in his black Yamaha with the big dragon artwork on it. It was a big, almost jumbo-sized guitar. I used it on that song because it gave the sound he wanted on that track.

The day before we cut 'Beautiful Boy' he said, 'I'm bringing another acoustic in for you to use.' I loved my J-45 and said, 'Well, I'll try it.' When he showed up the next day with that guitar, I took one look at it and, before I'd even played it, I thought, 'I'm going to use that!'

I've gotta say, though, I was pretty fucked up around that time with John. I'd been high since I was fifteen years old, but now, in 1980, at twenty-seven, I was in bad shape.

It didn't alter anything about my behaviour though, and I wasn't trying to hide anything. I just went about my business.

The Hit Factory, at the time, stocked my beer in the beer closet, and I was the only one that drank it. The studio featured stacks of Rolling Rock bottles everywhere at the end of the sessions. Rolling Rock didn't seem to get me as fucked up as the other beers, so that was my idea of taking it easy. I could drink two dozen of those fucking things a day without falling on my head. Plus, I had a constant supply of blow.

The thing is, we all say, 'Back in the day, it didn't really affect my playing,' but I'm not sure if it did or it didn't. I have no fucking idea. I like what I played on that record, though. As a matter of fact, if I wasn't high then, I couldn't play. If anything, my drug and alcohol use might have stunted the growth of my playing, but it didn't affect my chops.

John made mention of it one time. I came in so fucking hungover and trashed that it was pretty obvious the condition I was in. Actually, it was a day off for me because they were going to do some percussion overdubs or something – stuff they didn't need the band for – but I had nothing to do that day, so I went by the studio to hang out.

When I walked in, John took one look at me and said, 'Had a good night out, did we?' I told him I had, but I could see his wheels turning as I was telling him about the previous night's exploits.

Pretty soon, John said, 'You know what? Just for giggles, we're going to do some hand claps.' Well, imagine what that's like, sweating and hungover and trashed doing hand claps? I was John's entertainment. I think it made his day because he wasn't using anymore, so he could look at me and think, 'Yup, that's why I don't do that shit.'

Working with John was a completely different experience to working with David Bowie. First of all, it was a bigger band, and it was all seasoned session guys. With David, we would end up with a core band of a bass player, two guitar players and a drummer, based around the live band, and whatever happened after that – whatever overdubs were done later – happened. Whereas with John, we had two guitar players, a bass player, a drummer, a percussionist and a keyboard player, plus John and Yoko. He was trying to capture a lot. But it was all there right away, too, so it was all recorded like that. When we were recording the basic tracks, we would feel them out as a group, and then we'd do the overdubs individually with John.

When it came time to do my solos, it was just John, Huey and me. Obviously, I'd worked with David like that, too, working out the solos, and he'd play one-on-one, eyeball to eyeball, so that part of it was similar. But the rest of it wasn't, mainly because we were working live and we were working sane hours. We didn't work on the weekends; just Monday to Friday, from eleven in the morning until about eight o'clock in the evening. That was it. And that was with a full hour for lunch – which came catered from a really good restaurant, usually sushi – just like working a regular job.

It created a convivial atmosphere, and it really gave everybody a chance, as part of an entire group where nobody was special, and where everybody felt equal. Nobody got special treatment. Obviously, everybody's relationship was unto itself with John, and everybody was a little different than the next guy, but even after the sessions were over, after I'd gone back to Los Angeles, I kept in touch with John by phone. He told me how things were progressing, and how the music had been well received once it hit the record stores.

Most of all, he kept reminding me that we would be hitting the road in 1981. 'See you soon,' he'd say.

On stage with Yoko performing songs we first recorded in
1980/81 for *Double Fantasy* and *Season of Glass*.

9

Without John

I heard the news in LA. John Lennon had been murdered in front of his apartment building, Yoko at his side, by some deranged nutjob.

The immediate aftermath was so intense. John had such big plans. The tour, the release of Yoko's groundbreaking single 'Walking on Thin Ice'. He'd wanted to know how people in LA were reacting to the record and then, in an instant, John was gone.

Instead of talking to him on the phone, I watched the world mourn the man I had admired from afar before becoming his friend. I was headed back to New York for the holidays. Frankly, it was the last place I wanted to be.

Early in 1981, Yoko called. We had a warm conversation. She was bereft, obviously, but she wanted to know how I was. That amazed me, considering what had happened. Pretty soon, I stopped by the Dakota to say hello and to see how she was doing. The mood was sombre, but I could tell she really appreciated I came by.

On my visits, we'd sit around and have a couple of drinks and talk easily about things. One time, much to my surprise, she brought up going back into the studio with the same band – the exact crew that recorded *Double Fantasy*. I could see the sense in it.

In February 1981, after I'd just gotten back to LA, the office called and said Yoko was ready to get back into the studio to make what would become the *Season of Glass* album. I didn't even hesitate. I needed it. I was on the next plane.

There were new songs written – 'Goodbye Sadness', 'Even When You're Far Away' and 'I Don't Know Why' – alongside songs I remembered right away from the original sessions with John. Yoko had some demos she'd recorded, and she'd written out chord charts for us. So, we put it together, one piece at a time.

We never talked about it directly, but the sessions, with all the original guys, in the same studio, and those songs – both the old ones and the new ones – must have been some kind of therapy. It was Yoko's way of dealing with the tragedy. And I think to get us all back together again, to make a record, was, in her mind, a healing thing for the whole group of us, who were all pretty shattered by what had happened.

The only thing that changed was the producer. Instead of Jack Douglas we had Phil Spector. And it turned out to be a nightmare.

On one of my visits to the Dakota after John died, Yoko brought up the people she was thinking of working with, and she mentioned Phil. At the time I was excited about the idea. That feeling lasted *at most* twenty-four hours after I first met him. Then I realized we were involved with one of the craziest motherfuckers that I'd ever met in my life.

On the first day we came in and before he arrived, Yoko played us some of the stuff. We started putting the arrangements together and because we had a musical director, just like on *Double Fantasy*, he started working on updating her charts for the guys, while I just kind of listened and learnt.

Then Spector came in, and it was like Satan himself had walked into the room.

Let me set the scene. Here we were, in the middle of winter, and it was freezing outside and colder inside. He had the control room air conditioning set below zero. It was also pitch dark. With all the lights out in the main studio, when you looked through the glass into the control room all you saw were the pilot lights on the machines. Like some weird *Close Encounters* light show.

Spector didn't deal with anyone directly. It was all through a third person. He would speak through Lee DeCarlo, our engineer. He didn't care to learn our names or if he knew them, he never used them. We were reduced to our roles.

'Tell the guitar player on the left-hand side of the room to play this.'

'Tell the bass player to speed up.'

The directives came through the intercom as a disembodied voice. We could have been in different states, not mere yards apart. It was as different a vibe from working with Jack, and especially with John, as it possibly could have been, and as cold as fuck however you looked at it.

I never made any sense of Spector's process. We couldn't get anything solid done because he was doing it in pieces. After working with John, we were used to playing together live as a band. John sat in the room and played the songs with us, then told us to our faces what he liked and didn't like. We got really tight.

In contrast, Spector would record one drum at a time, one guitar at a time. Sometimes he'd record a few of us together, but he'd have us do it over and over, take after take, on top of what we'd already done, with limited feedback. It wasn't making sense to any of us. Musically it felt disjointed and incomprehensible.

Outside of the studio and control room in a small sitting area, he had a big deli tray of cold meats and snacks brought in. We were told it was hands off except for Spector. None of us could touch anything on it. Now, this area was near the bathroom so all of us passed that tray several times a day. I couldn't have been the only one wrestling with the temptation to snag a cheese square, but none of us ever did, which speaks to the unease and weirdness in the air.

Strangely enough, Spector never took a bite of a single item on the tray, even though he insisted that it be fresh, every day, no matter what. On top of that, the control room was stocked with Tropicana orange juice half-gallon bottles – the glass ones with the indentation for you to pick it up – each pumped full of Sangria wine. Each had two straws in it. The display of Sangria always sat on the recording console. Or else! At some point in the day, I'd think about taking a cool sip of Sangria, but the urge was never enough to set foot in there. The vibe was freaky.

Spector had a bodyguard with him, a hulking monster who followed him around. If he left the studio to go to the bathroom or the lounge, Godzilla would get there first to clear not only the area but also the path to get there. But in a way the bodyguard did us a favour. None of us wanted to run into Spector by accident or, God forbid, talk to him.

I admit to drinking at times while recording, but Spector took it to another level. Not only was he drunk, he walked around with a Dirty Harry shoulder holster and a fucking .44 Magnum long barrel stuffed in it.

Remember, this was just a few weeks after John had been shot down in the street. I wasn't too out of it to think 'This is fucking surreal.' And wrong. All of it was wrong. Yoko seemed to be in a fog. Understandably so. None of us wanted to bother her with our misgivings. Then, one day, she and I arrived at the Hit Factory at the same time. We got in the elevator together, just the two of us, and I asked, 'What time is he coming in today?'

'He's not coming in today,' she said. 'You won't be seeing him anymore.' That marked the beginning and the end of any conversation we ever had about Phil Spector.

He hadn't lasted two weeks. And it was still way too long.

The other controversy surrounding *Season of Glass* was the album cover. I had an early glimpse on one of my visits to see Yoko at home. She showed me the photo she'd taken of John's bloody glasses, just the way they were when the hospital returned them to her after John was murdered.

'What do you think about this as an album cover?' she asked.

'You're going to get a lot of heat,' I told her. She asked me again, 'What do *you* think?'

Typical Yoko. She doesn't let you skate.

'I think it's appropriate,' I said. 'You're making a state-ment with that cover. No matter what you do, the fact that you're even making a record this soon, or at all, and know-ing the way the press is, it could go sideways regardless of what you do. If this is what you want to say, say it.'

I wasn't telling her anything she didn't already know.

Like clockwork, the album became a flashpoint of con-troversy, so much so that the record company approached her about changing the cover because it was hurting sales. They said record shops didn't stock it saying it was in 'bad taste'. You know what's bad taste? Not fucking acknow-ledging that someone was gunned down in cold blood.

Later, in the liner notes to her *ONOBOX* box set, Yoko wrote of feeling like she was 'Soaked in blood coming into a living room full of people and reporting that my hus-band was dead, his body was taken away, and the pair of glasses were the only thing I had managed to salvage – and people looking at me saying it was in bad taste to show the glasses to them.'

'I'm not changing the cover. This is what John is now,' is what she said to the record executives.

With Spector gone, work on the album took off. We were doing five days a week, seven or eight hours, max, just like when we did *Double Fantasy*. We started at ten or eleven in the morning and finished up by seven or eight in the evening, with a break for lunch. The whole band ate together like we did with John and Yoko, just a few months earlier, having a proper meal – sushi was a regular – before going back for the afternoon shift.

Things felt like they were back to normal except, of

course, they weren't. Every day when we wrapped up with Yoko, I would remember how after John's sessions were over, he would have Lee DeCarlo, the engineer, make him a rough mix of the day to take home. I'd hang around with him while he waited because John would tell stories and jokes. That's how it was every evening. I missed the lilt in his voice before the punchline to a funny story; I loved that he loved making us laugh. Now, the absence of that good-natured coda to the day cut deep. Instead, the session done, I'd head out into the cold, grey New York night.

Even though it was the same group of guys, who had all gotten really close with John in the time we'd been working with him, we didn't talk about him all that much. We just focused on what we were doing. The sessions felt like one of the days when John was out of the studio doing interviews or something. You'd have been hard-pressed to tell the difference. With crazy Phil gone, progress came quickly.

Finally, with the basic tracks recorded, I stayed at the studio late into the evenings with Yoko, often for hours, putting on overdubs and solos just like I had on 'Kiss Kiss Kiss' and other songs on *Double Fantasy*.

Yoko knew I could do the more out-there things. I was really engaged. Occasionally, we ended up back at the Dakota after these sessions because she wanted to go over the day's work to make sure the arrangements and what we had cut were working. But mostly, I think she just needed somebody around. I'd go back to the apartment with her and we'd listen to the tapes Lee had given her of the day's work, and we'd talk. Even when we went back to the Dakota during those late nights, there was not a lot of talk of John.

It was about the music. 'What are we going to do tomorrow? How are these arrangements?' That kind of thing.

Eventually, late into the night, she'd send for a limo. Two armed bodyguards would take me back to my hotel, which was on the opposite side of Central Park from the Dakota. She was taking no chances.

Before we started the sessions, it didn't occur to me that Yoko might be in danger, even with what had happened. But her insistence on armed guys being with me – these guys were the real deal and armed to the teeth – made me think about the stress and pressure she was under, on top of the tremendous grief of it all, and raising Sean now all on her own.

On 30 March, in the middle of the *Season of Glass* sessions, Ronald Reagan was shot. After what had just happened to John, it rattled everybody's cage. We got the news after the sessions wrapped for the day. My thoughts turned immediately to Yoko. I knew the shooting would hit her like a ton of bricks because of the unavoidable similarities to John's death. Not surprisingly, she cancelled the sessions for the next day.

A year after we did *Season of Glass*, Yoko planned to make another album. Back then, when you worked with an artist with a decent budget, if you wanted to use your own gear, it was no big deal. They just shipped it to wherever you were recording. Everything had road cases, mind you, so I sent it all out to New York. The day before I was supposed to leave, I got a phone call from Yoko's office. The person on the line said, 'Yoko is a bit embarrassed by this, but she did your numbers, and they're not working for this album.'

John and Yoko were heavy into numerology; Yoko still was. My reading had come up as not auspicious for that moment. I understood. Every artist has their own way of working, and I love Yoko. That said, my gear had already shipped. I had to get my gear back. When the shipping company dropped it at my house, I noticed two giant fork-lift holes through the case that had the AC30 in it. I opened the case up and the amp was trashed. The forklift had gone right through the head of the amp. I guess Yoko was right about the numbers.

I never replaced the AC30, but Yoko did make good on the dough for it. Also, because the gig was cancelled last minute, she made good by sending me a cheque for five grand with an apology: 'Sorry it didn't work out this time.'

Yoko was always a class act.

I don't sit around thinking about the relatively brief time I spent working with and getting to know John and Yoko, but occasionally something pops up on YouTube – a Beatles clip, usually – and I'll think, 'Holy shit! I got to work with one of the most amazing artists in history.' Working with John took about eight weeks out of my life. It wasn't like working with David, with whom I worked for decades and got to see him change and evolve, not only as an artist but as a person, even becoming a dad.

Like David, John was a remarkably normal guy. You didn't have to walk on eggshells around him. As famous as he was – let's face it, the Beatles went through something unlike anything that anyone else had experienced – John was incredibly grounded. He made it easy to work with him and get to know him, but I marvel at how the kid from that little house in Liverpool turned into the guy who took The Beatles to the cultural mountaintop, wrote 'Give Peace a Chance' and 'Imagine' and did countless other things first at a level for a rock-and-roll band that no one else – not David, not the Stones – could do.

After getting that note from Yoko, though, I was done with New York. I headed back to Los Angeles.

On stage with David and Carlos Alomar during
the 1983 Serious Moonlight Tour.

10

Serious Moonlight

One morning, in the spring of 1983, I got home from taking my daughter to school and Jean said, 'You got a phone call that sounded kind of important. Some guy named Wayne Forte.'

'Are you kidding me? That's David's booking agent.' When I called him back, Wayne cut to the chase.

'We've got a situation,' he said. David was in Brussels doing dress rehearsals for his new tour. Stevie Ray Vaughan, the up-and-coming Texas bluesman who'd signed on as David's lead guitarist for the tour after they'd worked together on David's latest album, *Let's Dance*, had quit, and David wanted – or really *needed* – me back in the band.

'When do you need me there?'

'Now.'

I didn't respond right away. Trying to gauge just how badly they needed me, I said, 'They're halfway around the fucking world and my passport expired about a week ago.'

Wayne said, 'No problem. Let me make some phone calls.'

He called me back almost right away and said he had my passport and visa sorted out. I had all the paperwork the following morning, and I took it all to the downtown courthouse and I got everything in order. The next day I was on a plane. It was four days before the first gig of what would be David's mammoth Serious Moonlight Tour.

I'd put together that things were 'code red' when I saw just how fast Wayne had pulled everything together. When they told me that David was doing gigs in four days, even though I hadn't been keeping up with any of what had been going on, I knew it was an emergency, no doubt about it.

While we were recording *Double Fantasy*, David was doing *The Elephant Man* a few blocks away on Broadway, but we didn't even cross paths during any of the time I was working with John. Afterwards – and after making Yoko's record and going back to make *Silver Condor* – my gut told me my band was going to implode. I could feel it. But it was feeding my family. It was a survival thing. I had to do what I do. I had to keep playing to make a living. But even though there was a considerable advance, and we were touring, and we had tour support, I was not happy. Not one fucking bit. When I did leave, I faced a void living in LA because there wasn't a lot going on. I went back and forth to New York on and off in '81 into '82, and at the beginning of '83.

Meanwhile, unbeknownst to me, *Let's Dance* was released. Right away, it was a massive hit. But I wasn't paying attention. I hadn't heard anything from anybody in David's camp, so I had no idea, really, what he was doing, and frankly didn't give him a thought. Hearing from his office that morning, after walking my daughter to school, was one of those weird moments where it really did feel like things were aligning in a way I hadn't imagined. Within forty-eight hours, I was on a plane to Brussels.

It was so rushed that they hadn't even sent me music to learn before I left for the airport. Every minute, from the first phone call from Wayne until the time I got on the plane, was spent sorting out my passport and travel arrangements.

As soon as I landed in Brussels, and checked into the hotel the band was staying at, a knock came on the door. It was David.

I hadn't seen David since all the ugly business at the end of 1975. We'd had no contact that entire time. Not a word. But he walked in, seeming quite happy to see me, and said, 'Let's go out and have a coffee.'

We settled in at an off-the-beaten-path café, so while people recognized him, they left us alone. Europe, especially then, was different.

I remember this clear as a bell. We both said at the same time something like 'We're going to have to clear the air before we get going.' Then David told me his version of events, and I told him my version. As it turned out, we'd both gotten played. Management fed both of us bad information to pit us against each other. I believed David's side of the story, and David believed mine, because it made so much sense, and things were cleared up over the first coffee.

One thing about David was he didn't play games. That's the way he operated. If, in fact, it was all bullshit, there never would have been a 'let's go clear the air' conversation. It never would have happened. There'd have been no reason for the rigmarole.

Meanwhile, David looked really, really healthy. We were both in good shape at the time. We caught up, and joked around about old times, and after all the making up was done, he said, 'We're in dress rehearsals. We've got four days left. We're doing a huge thing called the US Festival in California in two weeks. We're under the gun here. Can you have this shit really together within the next two weeks?'

I was surprised. Wayne had told me the first show was in four days.

'No,' I said. 'I can have it together for the first show.'

I soon realized what David was talking about. The US Festival in San Bernardino was a huge outdoor festival put on by Steve Wozniak of Apple Computers, who'd built a state-of-the-art open stadium for the occasion. Each day of the festival featured different music categories. The Clash and INXS kicked off the festival on Saturday – New Wave Day. Van Halen, Judas Priest, Mötley Crüe and other heavy-metal bands headlined Sunday. On Memorial Day, David was billed alongside U2, Los Lobos and The Pretenders. And the following Saturday, Willie Nelson and Hank Williams, Jr closed the event. The festival expected more than half a million people. I understood why David was panicked.

Pretty soon, I got a list of the songs I had to know. I only knew half the material! David had made a lot of albums in that interim period when I was gone. I wrote the songs down in a long list, and then I wrote out little chord charts next to each one. I had a palm-size cassette recorder and I just kept playing the songs. And playing them. And playing them. I stayed up for four days working everything out. Sleep was not an option.

I had a safety net in Carlos. He spent a lot of time with me in my room, showing me the bits and pieces from the stuff that I'd never played on before, which helped me out quite a bit. And on those first couple of shows, he really saved my ass by holding it all together.

We had a fairly even workload because Carlos was handling a lot of the soul-style songs that we'd recorded for *Young Americans* in Philadelphia in the summer of 1974, and I was handling the Ziggy stuff and all the more rock-and-roll-oriented guitar work.

On a personal level, we always had a little underlying friction, but even with that our families would hang out together. During the Serious Moonlight period, our daughters, who were about the same age, and our wives, who were both music business pros in their own right, became close, so we'd fly them out occasionally. Like when we played Anaheim Stadium, they came out for the week and we took the kids to Disneyland.

It did get ugly at times. Like in any band, the atmosphere could get testy. The competitive nature inside the framework of the organization breeds it. With Carlos being designated the musical director on the Serious Moonlight Tour, our clashing was just waiting to happen. As much as I like to think I'm a bigger man, I'm not, and I got sucked into the drama and acted like a real asshole at times. So, we had a very odd relationship but we figured out how to make it work because, like on *Young Americans* and *Station*, our roles were clearly defined and it wasn't like we were both scrambling for the same spot.

Back in the trenches, on the opening night of the Serious Moonlight Tour, in Brussels, I would say that during about 25 per cent of the show I either laid out or made mistakes, but 75 per cent of it was on the money. Brussels was a good place to start a European tour. It was low key and out of the spotlight. By the time we got to the US Festival, I was on it.

My relationship with David felt different this time around. I was treated with more respect than I was before. I was given much more room to move on stage. I wasn't told what to do. And when he tried to dress me up, I said, 'That shit sucks. I ain't wearing that.' 'Ah, same old Slicky, I see,' he replied, and we laughed.

So, I was the only member of the band who was not in uniform. I ended up wearing Stevie Ray Vaughan's clothes. Stevie – who had quit the tour at the last minute, and who probably had 75 pounds and 2 inches in height on me – had left behind a cool pink-and-black checked shirt and a pair of parachute pants. I added the green suspenders – to hold the damn things up – but David had all of this heavy jewellery shit, from out of *Jason and the Argonauts*, and I said, 'Nope. I ain't wearing that shit.' I got my own boots and that was it. He left me alone.

There wasn't a lot of talk about Stevie at the time because everybody focused – especially David – on the show coming together. Gossip and hearsay – there wasn't any room for it. David didn't ever have room for that crap, anyway. Ever. It wasn't his thing. If he got pissed off about something, he vented and that would be the end of it.

Of course, I'd heard Stevie Ray Vaughan's name, but he hadn't really broken out yet. He was a household name in Texas, but I became aware of him after hearing what he'd done with David and Nile Rodgers on *Let's Dance*. When I started listening and learning the songs for the tour, I remember thinking, 'Wow, this is a great mix that David's got on here,' because he had Nile Rodgers playing the rhythm part and Stevie's bluesin' all over it. Brilliant. It worked so incredibly well because it was such a pop record – and definitely not your usual, edgy David Bowie album – and Stevie's contribution brought it back to the street and away from being a synthesized pop album.

The thing about it was with the way Stevie played against the way David was *thinking* at the time. I guarantee that there aren't too many guitar players that would've come in there and, off the cuff, done what he did without some kind of direction from the boss man. Period. So, Stevie obviously understood where David was at. When it did come time for me to do the Serious Moonlight Tour, having worked with David before and David knowing that the way it worked was that I'd never tried to be Mick Ronson, so I wasn't going to try to be Stevie Ray Vaughan, I was just left to my own devices to do what I did. That was great. Because as much as I liked Stevie's playing, I can't play like that. He's a Texas blues player, atypical for sure, but still his roots are there. I'm more of an urban blues player, in the vein of B. B. King, Buddy Guy and Howlin' Wolf, which is very different.

So, I wasn't interested in why Stevie quit, or any other fucking thing. I just thought, 'Wow, I got my job back.' I was happy.

Back when we did the Diamond Dogs Tour, because of the whole Broadway stage production thing that David wanted, the musical director Michael Kamen, with his background from Juilliard and a knowledge of things that nobody else had a clue about, drastically changed some of the arrangements for that tour. If you listen to *David Live*, 'The Jean Genie' and 'All the Young Dudes' don't seem like the same songs as were on the original recordings. But when we got to Serious Moonlight, we went back to the studio albums. We drew from the basic arrangements from the original recordings. I liked that because I liked the original versions of most of David's songs, and because those arrangements for the Diamond Dogs Tour, while making it more theatrical, sucked the rock out of them. They were Broadway versions of Bowie songs, in my opinion, with all due respect to my pal, the late, great Michael Kamen.

Serious Moonlight, unlike the Diamond Dogs Tour, was all very First Class. We went from David staying in nice hotels and the band at Holiday Inns, to us all staying at top-notch hotels. We had a private jet – a 707 – which was gigantic. And there was an elaborate stage backdrop, with big columns that would fill up with smoke, and a fantastic light show. It didn't match the spectacle of the Diamond Dogs Tour, but it was still amazing.

And in that time, David graduated from arenas to stadiums, which was a hell of a jump. We had an amazing top-notch crew, and everybody in the band got along well. They were all new guys that I wasn't familiar with, except Carlos. The level of it all was completely different and it was, certainly in hindsight, a more enjoyable tour for me.

Plus, we had a truly great drummer. For me, it's always the drummer who is the most important connection for me onstage because that's the main person I feed off. It's totally visceral. When I don't like the drummer, I don't like the drummer. Because if I can't feel that primal shit coming out of a drummer, I can't play. But if I've got a good one, I can play the shittiest gig in the world and be happy. Tony Thompson had a great sense of humour, too, and he was clever at inserting levity when it was most needed, say in the middle of a heated argument. So, I did spend a lot of time by the drum kit, which was easier to do than it was with Sterling Campbell, who was David's drummer towards the end of his touring days, because of the way the stage was set up later on, when Sterling wasn't in the centre the way Tony was. Sterling was off to stage left a bit, and even though I'd go back there, I didn't like the idea of crossing behind David when he was in front, unless I felt like it was the right time to do it.

David, meanwhile, was more accessible and no longer dealing with the demons that had possessed him during the end of the first period I'd worked with him. We were still all doing drugs, of course. But maybe because the schedule was gruelling – although manageable because everything was taken care of so you didn't have to do much except play – and because these weren't short shows, it didn't get out of hand like in the old days. But mostly David was healthier, and happier. Finally, he was getting the money that he deserved. The money that he'd lost and the money that was stolen from him earlier on was coming back a hundredfold.

It was an upbeat period. I spent more time with David during our off-hours. That separation that had always existed between him and the band lifted. He was easy-going, and he wasn't anything like he was during that whole crazy 'Thin White Duke' time. That was gone. Here was a guy that you could actually have a conversation with. We would talk about what was going on with the band or what was in the news. Just shit that two guys travelling together and working together might talk about.

I got to really like him. Most of all, it was easy to work with him because at least I knew who the hell I was working with. Before, from day to day, I didn't know.

Not surprisingly, the shows demonstrated the professionalism and ease of the band.

Two weeks flew by and I felt more than ready for the US Festival. We flew to the States just to do that gig. We hopped on a plane in Europe and disembarked in sunny Palm Springs. We settled in at our hotel and had one day to get rid of the jet lag.

On that day off, David and I did a photo shoot. Just the two of us, with the photographer Denis O'Regan. We spent the whole afternoon out in the desert. My favourite shot is of me and David standing in an abandoned cinder-block building, with him in the background and me up front. And there's another shot of the two of us sitting on some rocks.

At the US Festival, David was the headliner. Once we arrived at the festival site, the first thing that struck me was the sheer size. From the stage, I couldn't see where the audience ended. It just kept going. Right over the horizon;

it was a sea of people. You don't realize the scale of things until after they're over. But this wasn't just another gig. We were headlining the biggest festival on the planet. Of course, I wasn't making any more than my normal weekly salary, but this was huge for David.

After we finished the show, we got cars that took us straight to the airport runway where we got on our plane. We had to sit on the ground awaiting clearance for a while, so David brought on a sushi chef. Next thing we knew, the wheels were up and we were on our way back to England.

We did Wembley Arena and the NEC Birmingham, then Paris, Sweden and Germany. The festival in Paris drew 120,000 people, and a couple of the shows were multiple dates that added up to a lot of people, but none of them compared to the US Festival, that's for sure.

Then we did shows at Milton Keynes in England. Over three nights we played to almost 200,000 people. Check out any of the photos, and you'll see how amazing those shows were. They weren't a festival gig. This was a David Bowie gig, not that far from where he grew up. Everyone came to see him. It was like a coming home.

But funnily enough, the show most memorable to me took place the night before at the Hammersmith Odeon, which holds 2,100 people. We all got a case of the jitters! Not at the big gig – Milton Keynes – but at the Hammersmith Odeon. It was weird. I remember being backstage pacing around like a fucking caged animal, and there was David, pacing along right next to me. That used to happen at Madison Square Garden for some reason, too. We used to joke about it when we did the Garden. 'Why does this happen every time we play here?' Come on. LA is 'blah blah blah,' but New York City is fucking New York City. And the Garden is the Garden.

But I do remember both of us having a case of the nerves something awful for the Hammersmith Odeon gig. And then the next day, standing in front of a sea of people being perfectly okay. But that little room, with 2,100 people, was frightening.

About a week later, we headed to North America. Between mid-July and mid-September we did about fifty dates, all in a row, one after the other. These were all sell-outs, to about 15,000 people, except for a few later on that were stadium shows in Hershey, Foxborough and Oakland. All sellouts, too.

It's hard to explain because the numbers don't lie, but it felt absolutely normal. This is where we are, and this is where we're supposed to be right now. There was no conscious thought put into it whatsoever about how big everything was getting. Zero. I really didn't think about it. I just did it. I understand that is something that is very hard for somebody to digest that wasn't there. But it wasn't until later on, in hindsight, that I could look at it and go, 'Holy shit. That was ridiculous.' But I guess it's because I was really comfortable. Put it this way: I knew that every night when I got on the stage, I didn't have to worry about anything, like equipment breaking or guitars being out of tune. I didn't have to do anything except show up and play. That's all I had to do. Because of the amount of revenue generated, we could have these creature comforts, and this crew that was so efficient, that we didn't have to think about anything but the show. And once you've done enough shows in a row, the whole thing is almost on autopilot.

Of course, I do remember certain nights, like on any tour, where we'd all agree, 'Wow, we really kicked ass tonight.' Or 'Eh, not sure if that show was that good.' But that's just the normal everyday stuff of touring. That never changes. But it definitely wasn't until later on that I appreciated the scale of the whole thing.

When we got to the end of the first leg of the tour, the break was a real break. There was no recording here and there, like during the Diamond Dogs Tour. Everybody went their separate ways and chilled out, and then we resumed. What got me really stoked was that we were going to Japan, Singapore, Hong Kong, Australia and New Zealand, parts of the world I'd never played before with anybody.

Over there, David's reception bordered on Beatlemania, though it surprised me how quiet the Japanese audiences were.

When we got to Hong Kong, it was 8 December, exactly three years after John had died. David had been close to John, and he knew how I felt about John, so it was still raw for both of us.

When you are involved with a tour like that, you don't live in the real world. You're sealed in a mysterious bubble sequestered from everything. Maybe on a day off you might think, 'Hey, we're in Singapore, man, let's go out and do something really cool.' But I remembered that anniversary coming up. All of a sudden, a couple of days before, we both realized it at the same time. 'Holy shit. You realize that date that we're ending the tour on?' We agreed, 'Well, we've got to do something.' I suggested 'Across the Universe' because it was one of my favourite John Lennon songs and because we had recorded it with John for *Young Americans*.

It seemed appropriate. It felt like the right song to do.

But David decided 'Imagine' would be better.

We worked it up at soundcheck. By that time the band was really good, and super tight. We could learn anything in five minutes, especially when you're talking about a song like 'Imagine', which you've heard six million times.

It was an emotional performance, and I remember it for a number of reasons. It was the anniversary of John's death, of course. But also, I didn't want the tour to end. I really didn't. I felt close to tears the whole night. And when David sang 'Imagine', it was one of the most gut-wrenching four minutes I've ever spent onstage. I don't think anybody in the band could even look at each other. It wasn't just because of the song we were doing. It was surreal that we were doing a tribute to our hero, who'd been taken away from us so unexpectedly and in such a heinous way. Those thoughts go through your head, of course. But all of a sudden, it's not just the tour that was over, you're realizing that John was over, too. It all filled my mind while I was playing the song.

It was an incredibly emotional moment for everyone to leave that tour on.

That night, David's team organized an after-show tour-ending party at this elaborate private place. It was huge, decked out in beautiful Chinese art everywhere, with

Chinese dance performances and musical performances, plus a huge dinner with lots of people. It was a great, fun night.

In my hotel room afterwards packing, I looked out of the window at the lights of Hong Kong, thinking, 'Wow. It's over.' It was hard to process because after spending so long in the bubble, the outside world didn't feel real. I was going to get on a plane the next day and fly back to the West Coast. Even that – which is normal, really – felt surreal.

That feeling was an unspoken thing among the band. I don't think any of us wanted to engage in that conversation. We'd had a blast at the party, and then everybody went back to their rooms to get packed up. We talked back and forth on the phone that night while packing and banging on each other's doors and all that, but we weren't talking about things like the tour being over. The next day, we got on a plane and we all left.

One thing I remember like it was yesterday is David saying, 'The beginning of the year is coming up, and I'm going to make a record. Just be ready for January.'

So, there I was in January, but the phone sure wasn't ringing. I thought, 'What the fuck is going on?' And then I got a call from Carmine Rojas, David's bass player at the time, saying that they were in the studio cutting the *Tonight* album. I was never given a date, a time, nothing. Zero. I wasn't fired or anything. Nobody called me.

Of all the times that David and I ended something when he'd disappear or wouldn't call me or fired me, that instance really got me and pissed me off. We all did a helluva job on the Serious Moonlight Tour. He was happy as hell. We all were. If you look at the footage of those shows, or any of the photos of us interacting on that tour, the chemistry is off the charts. I felt like I'd been slapped in the face.

Then the phone rang.

John Waite, hot off the back of his hit single, 'Missing You', needed a guitar player.

Left: With Slim Jim Phantom and Lee Rocker. *Right:* Playing with Carl Perkins' band alongside Eric Clapton, George Harrison and Ringo Starr.

MTV, Keith and More Beatles

John seemed like a cool guy, and right away asked me to put a band together for the tour. My first call was to Carmine Rojas, fresh out of the *Tonight* sessions.

I'd met Carmine, who was David's bass player throughout much of the 1980s, for the first time in Brussels, Belgium, for the rehearsals for the Serious Moonlight Tour. He stood out because he went out of his way to make me feel comfortable as the guy being thrown into that fire at the last minute. We became really good friends, and almost like family. After a year on tour with David, there was an understanding between us. And just as well, because my drug habit was getting worse.

Sometimes I wouldn't eat for a ridiculously long amount of time, but he would be there, knocking on my hotel room door in the middle of the night, his arms full of protein and carbs, and he'd sit there and watch me eat. If it was one of those days when I was seriously out there, he'd keep an eye on me. He was definitely the brother that I needed because I was on pretty shaky ground at that point.

In New York City on a week off between gigs, I overdosed because my drug use at that time had gone through the roof. It was bad. I mean, there was a never-ending supply of cocaine. Also, at the time, I knew a couple of guys in the city that had really good heroin, so I'd use the heroin to come down from the coke. I was on a bad speed-ball run for a while. I don't know how much Carmine knew, and I sure as hell wasn't advertising it, but I think it was pretty obvious by looking at me. So, if it wasn't for Carmine, I might not have made it out of that tour alive. He was definitely the one to put the brakes on me when they needed stomping on. And I listened to him, which I didn't do with anybody else.

As a player, Carmine is a trip because there isn't any style that he can't do convincingly. It's not like a session guy who's reading charts. He *feels* the shit. When he was with Bowie, he felt that. When he was doing Rod Stewart, he felt that. When he was with Joe Bonamassa, he felt that. He knew how to become part of the feeling of the music, so he was not just playing the notes. As a stage performer, he looks great and really gets around on stage. And he's got charisma to spare.

Most of all, he was the voice of reason and the calm factor that was needed, no matter the band or situation. If the vibe started getting out of hand between a few guys, Carmine was the one that could somehow throw some cold water on that thing and get everybody to go to their corners.

The John Waite tour was fun – it's always great when you're supporting a hit record. Afterwards, we headed into the studio to record some demos for John's next album. We wrote a couple of tunes together, and I made a deal with his management, so I was really happy.

But as is almost always the case in the music business, the good times didn't last. Just as we were ready to go into a studio in Port Jefferson, New York, in early 1985, I got a call from John's management crying poverty, saying they had to cut my deal by a fair amount. I told them, 'Look, we had an agreement. It's on paper. You just sold 1.5 million albums and you had a Number 1 single, not to mention a successful tour that I was a huge part of. A deal's a deal.'

But they said they just couldn't afford what we'd agreed to, and that the rest of the band had already agreed to a pay cut. I listened, but it didn't take very long before I told them, 'You live up to what's on paper or find another guy for John to work with.'

It was a tough call, to be honest. I had a good deal. I had points and money. I deserved it because it was my band that was out with John anyway. So, it wasn't really about the money.

Again, it was the principle of the thing. Again, I was out.

That's when I ran into Slim Jim Phantom and Lee Rocker at NAMM, the big West Coast industry trade show. Those guys had been the backbone of the Stray Cats, who were huge stars in the early 1980s, courtesy of MTV, just like John. Brian Setzer, the Cats' guitarist, had split up the band and gone off on a solo career, so they were looking for somebody to work with, and said they loved my playing and vibe and wanted to get together in Los Angeles to see how things might work between us.

We set up a rehearsal and I've got to admit, I was really looking forward to it. I saw Slim Jim and Lee as the real deal and felt I could definitely add exactly what they needed to the mix.

The first day there, I got in early, as always, and was sitting working out my guitar setup. That's when Slim Jim and Lee showed up. We said hello and chatted, and it turned out they'd already made some demos and had a deal in line with EMI. They said, 'The Cats are done and we've got this thing. What do you think?'

I said, 'It's worth a shot. Let's play.'

Right from the first day at the rehearsal place in LA, the chemistry clicked. Phantom, Rocker & Slick inked the deal with EMI.

The stuff the guys had already demoed was at least a starting point. The guitar player they'd used on them wasn't a bad guitar player, but there just wasn't any sparkle to the recordings. I added my thing – what I do – to what they'd already laid down. Immediately the tracks came to life.

I liked the way that Lee and Jim wrote songs, too. Jim did the lyric writing because he doesn't play guitar or anything. And Lee did all the musical arranging and came up with the melodies. Once the songs were fleshed out, they'd turn them over to me, so I could get the vibe. The record turned out great, and Stones-y as hell.

The material that they'd already written lent itself to that and then, once we came up with 'Men Without Shame', which turned out to be the single and eventually hit Number 7, we knew we were cooking.

Funnily enough, that song was a fluke and a half because that lick was something I had been playing at soundchecks during the Serious Moonlight Tour. It was one I'd had flying around, as you do once in a while, so I guess it could have ended up on *Tonight* if things had turned out differently. Instead, we got our own hit single out of it.

I played the lick at rehearsal one day and it got Jim and Lee's attention right away. So, we wrote the song, but we never even demoed the thing. We actually wrote it while we were recording the album, in one day, real quick. Still, I wasn't convinced about the song. In fact, Jim and Lee were on the fence, too, but I was *really* not convinced. But Steve Thompson, the producer, put his foot down. If it wasn't for him, we might not have polished off the song that became our big hit. After all those years of doing what I do, it still goes to show what I know.

It ended up in heavy rotation on MTV. The video we made was in the Top 10 for months on MTV. And the wanking guitar that opens the song ended up being used in the *MTV News* for about a year or two. They didn't have to pay for it because they used just enough underneath the legal limit to not have to pay me. But, you know, whatever. We sold a lot of records.

And then the second single made the Top 40, hitting Number 33 on the charts. That was 'My Mistake' with Keith Richards on it.

'My Mistake' had been demoed and I really liked it right away when Jim and Lee played it for me. I added what I thought would bring out the best of the song, and it ended up being probably one of the most Stones-y songs on the record. Seriously Stones-y after I got my hands on it. But that's why we do what we do for a living, and why people that don't get it always ask, 'How can you not know what's going to happen next?' But that's the beauty of my career. I live in a creative danger zone, where I'm either going to be fucked for a while or something's going to come out of nowhere that I never expected. And that's usually something that comes at me from a completely unexpected direction. That's what happened with 'My Mistake'.

Meanwhile, as we were wrapping up the first album, the phone rang. It was Steve Thompson, the producer. He told me he was in the studio with Mick Jagger, mixing 'Dancing in the Street', the song he'd recorded with David for Live Aid, and Mick did not like the guitars. He'd heard a couple of Phantom, Rocker & Slick tracks that Steve was mixing and asked Steve if he could get me in there to redo the parts he didn't like.

'Well, I'm coming in tomorrow, so I'll see you then.' But Steve interrupted me almost before I could finish. 'No,' he said, 'Mick wants you here now.'

'What do you mean now?'

'You've got to get a Red Eye,' Steve told me, and I knew he wasn't joking.

'Fuck, man. Come on. Give me a break.'

'Hold on,' Steve said, and Mick got on the phone.

'What's the problem?'

'There's no problem,' I said. 'But I've already got a flight booked.'

Mick, without missing a beat, said, 'Do I need to come over there on my bike and retrieve you and take you back to New York?'

We both laughed. I said, 'I'll be on the Red Eye.'

I was in the studio by eight the next morning. Mick was

already there. We started working right away, and I could tell he was happy.

Pretty soon, after hearing what was going on, he turned to me and Steve and said, 'Okay, you guys have got it. Just finish it up. I'm already good.'

We were shocked. But then, as he was making his way out of the control room door, he said, 'By the way, it's my birthday today. We're having a party at the Palladium. I'll make sure that your names are at the door.'

That's why he couldn't wait for me to get there on the Red Eye. You're welcome very much, Mick.

Mick's party was, of course, a big private event. In the men's room, who do I run into but Keith Richards. We ended up in a stall, doing what you do in there, dropping coke all over the floor, laughing a lot and having a great time. As we pulled ourselves together to head back out to the party, I said, 'You know, we're in the studio and there's a track on there that's got your name written all over it. Would you consider coming in and throwing something on there?'

Without missing a beat, Keith said, 'You got it.'

Meanwhile, we heard this voice calling to us. It was Ronnie Wood. Pretty soon we saw this nose coming over the top of the stall.

'What are you guys doing in there?'

Pretty soon the three of us squeezed into the stall.

True to his word, management set it up with Keith's people for him to come in. But at the appointed time, no Keith. He's going to show up sooner or later, right? But after a couple of days, still no Keith. Meanwhile, I already had a plane ticket booked and a commitment in the Virgin

Islands to be the best man at my buddy's wedding; a guy I grew up with. I couldn't stay. It was all planned, he'd bought me the ticket. Rooms were booked. Tuxedos had been organized. The whole nine yards. Every fucking thing had been taken care of. I couldn't stick around.

After waiting and waiting, as planned, I caught my flight. And sure as God made fucking green apples, the day after I got down there, Keith showed up at the studio.

What are the odds of this shit?

So, I wasn't there when Keith cut his parts. Everybody was there but me. They even got photos of Jim and Lee with Keith during the sessions.

I mean, it wasn't like I was worried that he wasn't going to deliver, or that he needed me there, because he was just going to do what he did. They just plugged him in, he did two takes, and then it was over. It wasn't like I was going to give him any direction or anything. When you call on Keith Richards, you just let him loose. You don't fucking even say anything to him. You don't even have to tell him what key it's in. You just send him in there and he does what he does.

It was nice having my name on there with his on a hit record, though. Because we sold a lot of records. And the funny thing is, if you take what we sold then, it would put us at Number 1 now for about a year.

During the course of making the album and all the promotional duties, and the long tour we did to support the record, Lee and Jim and I became really good friends. We got along great. Once we finished the tour, there was pressure right away from the record company to get back in the studio to do another record. They wanted to keep that momentum going. But it just doesn't work that way. Second records are tricky. It takes you your whole life to write the first one. Then they want the next one in a week. Between the pressure and the drugs, we started getting at each other's throats. And we ended up making a record that really sucked. And that was the end of the ball game. After finishing the album, we basically threw our hands up and called it a day.

We'd ended up with a producer we didn't want and we were getting too high. But really, someone should've told the suits at EMI, 'Hey, motherfuckers. Hold your horses. We cannot give you a record that's going to be acceptable that fast. Ain't going to happen.'

But for whatever reason, we let ourselves be pushed into doing it. The first record was actually recorded and mixed pretty quickly, of course, but the material was written already. What we really should have done was to get into a rehearsal room, gotten a good vibe on the tunes and a producer that worked for us.

It wasn't that things were bad. And it wasn't me feeling like a big star or anything. Sure, being sequestered in the David Bowie bubble I'd felt much more like a big shot. And because we were a three-piece band, really just starting out, we weren't travelling in a private jet. But we were selling records. We sure didn't have any worries, money-wise. We were fine. We were better than fine. And I really loved those guys. So it wasn't that. I think the combination of the disappointment that we felt in thinking that the record company could have done better by us and the rush into the studio when we weren't ready, on top of too many drugs and too much booze, was like being put in a blender. It seems obvious, but what do you get when all those things come together? You get a band that implodes.

Still, I had a lot of fun times during the Phantom, Rocker & Slick days.

For our first live show, on Halloween 1985, we got Cassandra Peterson in her Elvira getup to introduce us. We even had the great piano player Nicky Hopkins, who'd also played on the record, do that first show with us. By far the most exciting gig we played was when we played in the all-star tribute to one of the fathers of rock and roll, Carl Perkins. Now, Slim Jim and Lee were tried-and-true rockabilly cats. They got the call because of their association with Carl and Dave Edmunds, who was also on that show.

We flew to London at the end of '85 and ended up in a warehouse space on the water. The weather was nasty, but we rehearsed there for about four or five days. In fact, the rehearsals were the best part.

We were all in the room together – me, Slim Jim, Lee, Carl, Dave, Ringo Starr, Eric Clapton, George Harrison, Rosanne Cash – and I know you'll believe me when I say it was truly one of those out-of-body experiences. I felt like somebody had dropped me from one reality to another one. I looked around, and I thought, 'Jesus Christ. How did I get here? Ringo's behind me. Eric Clapton's here. George is there.' It was one of those moments when I stopped to say, 'Holy shit. This is seriously fucking cool.'

Carl was really fond of Slim Jim and Lee. Plus, Dave Edmunds had worked with them as well, so they were invited to participate, along with George Harrison and Ringo and everybody else, and so the invite was extended to the whole band. That's why I didn't get to play any electric on that show. All I played was an Ovation acoustic, which was rented. But as far as I was concerned, I was lucky just to be there. I didn't care what they asked me to do. As long as I was on a stage with those guys, give me a tambourine, even. I was happy. Besides, even Slim Jim didn't play drums on all of it. Ringo played a lot of those drum parts, as well he should have.

I'd heard George Harrison was reluctant to play live after The Beatles split up. And Ringo and Clapton, back in those days, didn't really show up for any old thing. The best part of the whole experience was that they were seriously into it. They had a blast. They loved Carl. If you watch the film of the show, there's footage of Carl kind of on his own, sitting on a stool doing a few tunes, and George comes over to him and he makes him do that really unique picking that he used to do, making slap-back echo without a pedal. George eggs him on to do it and if you watch it, and you look at George's face, and everybody's faces, really, it was all smiles.

We all got to hang out, too. At rehearsals, backstage, everything. That was really amazing. When we finished up and before we left, we were talking to George and he said, 'You know, I'm going to be in LA next month. Why don't I take you guys out to dinner?' I thought to myself, there's no way that's ever going to happen. But sure enough, not long after we got back home, my phone rang, then Jim's rang, and then Lee's. George called all of us, personally.

When I picked up the phone, he said, 'I'm here. How's tomorrow night?' I knew who it was right away, of course. We all went out to dinner. George booked an Italian restaurant. We dined in a little room in the back, just us, the wives, and George. I remember pulling up and George was pulling up at the same time. I was driving my '62 Studebaker Hawk, which I had completely restored – it was gorgeous – and George walked up to me and said, 'Man, that is a rock-and-roll car if ever I've seen one.' Talk about sitting on top of the world.

After that night, it all came crashing down.

I was in the twilight zone for about a year and a half because my drug use came to a head right around then. Until I got sober – in March 1988 – the period draws a complete blank. I had two kids up in Northern California with Jean. I was floundering around, doing stuff with a few people in the San Francisco area, but nothing that really turned into anything. It's all a haze.

Eventually, I drove down to LA. The whole way I said aloud, 'You're not going to drink. You're not going to drink.' But as soon as I got there, I went on a bender and a half. I thought, man, maybe some of these guys can keep going, but that ain't me. I've got to stop. I'm a dead man walking.

Circus Magazine ran photos from a benefit show at the Santa Monica Civic that I played. Guns N' Roses played, and then I joined an all-star band with some of the Heart-breakers from Tom Petty's band. It was great, I thought, until I saw the photos. The images were a wake-up call. I looked like I had just woken up from a week of drinking and drugging, which I probably had. I saw the magazine and within the hour, I called a buddy of mine who had been breaking my balls about getting into a programme. I said, 'You better come and get me. I think I'm done.' And that was it.

People talk about how hard it is to get clean, but after that, it was pretty easy for me. There was no hesitation. Once I made that phone call, there was no more fighting the urge. It was a long time coming, but I was ready to be done with that part of my life. I was very fortunate.

Of course, I had plenty of help. Somebody that I had met a few years earlier, unbeknownst to me, was in the programme. I was staying with this friend of mine who was a drinker, but I was going to meetings around the block and ran into this old friend. I told him about my situation, and he said, 'You've got to get out of there. You just can't be there. You can't.'

But I had nowhere to go.

'I have a room, and I have a friend who lives with me who works at a rehab, so he can help keep an eye on you.'

That's what I did. I detoxed there. I didn't even have rehab.

That solved the sobriety problem, but it didn't solve the rest of my life. I still had to get back on my feet. I had nothing. My gear was mostly sold. I was in debt. I had nothing left.

I managed to get a sizeable record deal within a year of getting sober, and a big publishing contract. The band I was working with was one that I knew I could get a deal with because it had the right ingredients. It wasn't the kind of band I wanted to be a part of and, once we signed, we were pushed even more in a direction that I didn't want to go. That was the Dirty White Boy band.

I wanted to do a real rock-and-roll, bluesy thing, like the Stones or the Faces. What I ended up with was a pop rock band. If you listen to the record today, it's not bad. It sounds good. The lead singer could sing his ass off. I was playing really well. It was just not my cup of tea. I tried to convince myself that it was, but in the end, my heart wasn't in it. We went out on the road, toured all over Europe and sold a lot of records there. But when we came back, we had a hard time getting the record released in the States. We had been signed by Dick Asher. He was a heavyweight motherfucker, who had been the legendary Walter Yetnikoff's right-hand man. Read the book *Hit Men*. He's all over that book. He was a sweet guy, too. We had everything in place: we had Dick, and we had a kick-ass team over at Polygram Records. But while we were in Europe, we got the news that a new president took over the helm of the label and our A&R guy, who had been great to us, lost all of his power during the internal drama that was going on.

Eventually, our manager got the label to put the record out, but they didn't do shit to support it. Zero. They pressed up a few copies and basically threw them out there. I finally got through to the new president and flat out asked him, 'What's going on? We're in limbo here. Our record's dead in the water.' He told me, 'Look, I just took this company over. You guys made two videos and a record and spent over $1 million. That is now on my tab. If I really put this company behind your record, I'm putting ownership on it. That means if it doesn't sell, I'm fucked. I'm sorry. That's not going to happen.'

And that was it.

'Is there anything holding me to this contract?'

He told me, 'Get a lawyer and we'll let you go.'

So, I did, and there weren't even any negotiations. The whole band was cut loose. The label wrote up some release forms and . . . bye-bye.

Honestly, the only reason I cared was because of the income. The other members seemed to be at each other's throats from day one, before we even signed the contract. I couldn't be around that shit. The constant fighting about money was just ridiculous. I was more than willing to go along and give it my best shot, but once it started to fall apart, there was really no reason to keep it together with a bunch of guys who appeared to be screaming at each other and fighting most of the time.

Before Dirty White Boy even imploded, I heard the band Little Caesar were having problems with their guitar player. I came in to cover some gigs because a good friend of mine was in that band, Loren Molinare. I'd known him for years. It was a solid rock band, not a hair band, which was hard to find at that time. Their audience was made up of bikers, and their first hit was a cover of the song 'Chain of Fools'.

When the second album came along, and they couldn't find another guitar player, I ended up signing to Geffen because they offered me a deal as part of the band. We made a record. We toured. And then the drug problems in the band pissed the record company off so bad that they dropped them.

In 1990 and 1991, I headed into the studio to record my *In Your Face* album. Terry Bozzio, the amazing drummer, played on the record. And Ron Young from Little Caesar sang on two of the songs. We recorded covers of 'Manic Depression' by Jimi Hendrix and 'A Change Is Gonna Come' by Sam Cooke. The Sam Cooke tune came out great. The rest of the album was instrumental. And for an instrumental record, it sold really well. It came out on a label called Metal Blade, run by Brian Slagel, who still owns the company and is one of the last men standing of those old indies.

But by the time 1992 rolled around, things weren't great. I was sober, thank God, but felt professionally adrift. The weariness seeped into my bones. So, what does a guitar-for-hire do when the embers burn low?

I started selling timeshares.

Top: Looking good with my friend's Shelby Cobra. *Bottom:* Not looking so good. But news reports of the car's demise prompted a reunion with David.

12

Sideman Turns Salesman

There was no place for me in LA. The guitar players getting hired for sessions were speed demons playing a million notes with no melody or soul. I couldn't have gone down that road even if I'd wanted to.

I drove to Lake Tahoe simply because it was beautiful country, with a plan to take whatever job came my way. I didn't give a shit if I was flipping hamburgers.

Almost right away I spotted an ad in the local paper. 'Make Millions!' it said. Sounded like bullshit but I went in for an interview. I passed all the personality and aptitude tests with flying colours, but they wanted a résumé. I was like a guy who'd just come out of prison. I had no professional past, as far as they were concerned. Then one of the guys running the tests recognized me and asked me what I was doing there. 'Things just fizzled out and I'm done,' I said. I told him the truth because I had nothing to lose and he told me he'd have a word with the boss.

I got the job. And I sucked really badly at it.

It was as though I'd broken into someone else's bad dream. Remember how I didn't want to wear the suit on stage that David had specially designed for me? Now, I had to wear one. Every. Day.

The people I worked for were crazier than any rock-and-roll band I knew. My bosses were supposed to be the masters of the universe, but some of them were doing more blow and drinking more than anyone I knew on tour. They'd come in dishevelled in the morning, with dark circles under their eyes and white powder on the tips of their noses, talking about how they'd gotten arrested over the weekend, but they'd be trying to hide how bad it was, too. It was insane. I kept thinking to myself, 'Seriously? I'm a black belt in this shit. You think I don't know what's up?'

The timeshares I was selling were serious multi-million-dollar affairs. Five-star across the board. I'm no dummy. I'm quick with business, and quick with my math. I can solve problems really fast. I'd had to master those things out of self-preservation doing what I had done up to that point in my life. But I found out in short order that it didn't do me a damn bit of good because I wasn't selling anything to high rollers. The people I was handed didn't have money to burn. My job was to convince them it was a buy-it-right-now thing. But it was an illusion. What I did seemed to be like stealing money from these motherfuckers. It made my skin crawl.

So, I sucked. And I got fired. I hit a couple more resorts. But they all fired me too. Then the guy who trained me told me, 'I've got an idea. We're short a manager and something tells me you'd kick ass at it.' Turned out I did. If someone else did the boring bit – what I thought of as the lying bit – I could close the deal. For the rest of the time at the resort, I was at the top of the sales numbers.

Prince's office called. This was a year before his famous

fallout with Warner Brothers and he changed his name to a symbol to piss them off. But I told his people, 'I've got a job, now. I'm not interested.' Same thing happened with Joe Cocker. I'd played with Joe before but turned him down flat. Then David Coverdale called and wanted me to go out on tour with him. I told him no, as well. At the time, these guys were some of the biggest stars on the planet, but I had my own thing going and I wasn't interested.

Meanwhile, I became friends with Mike Tramp, former frontman with the hair metal band White Lion. He'd moved out to Tahoe and was writing and playing singer-songwriter stuff with a Tom Petty vibe. He'd become friendly with some dot-com guys who made a killing and wanted to start a record label. Finally, something I understood that didn't require me to strap on a guitar. We called it Slick Ink. At the height of the CD boom, I called round old friends in the business and we re-released their old out-of-print albums.

I was starting to get antsy, though. Then, at the beginning of 1998, David Coverdale got back into town after wrapping up his tour and wanted to write and record a new album. I thought David was the real deal – he'd broken out big with his band Whitesnake and was still riding that wave – so I figured, at the very least, we'd have some fun. And maybe, just maybe, we'd make some hits.

I thought the material was really strong, but *Into the Light*, as the album was eventually called, wasn't the hit I thought it would be.

Then, just before Christmas 1999, I got a call from the Slick Ink webmaster telling me they'd gotten an email from someone at a company called ISO. Now, I'd never heard of the name of whoever sent the message, but I sure as hell knew what ISO was: that was David Bowie's company.

I called the number, and the woman who answered told me that David wanted to get in touch because he was producing a record and wanted me to play on it.

'What do you think?' she asked.

'Sure. Find out the details and keep me posted.'

It was just before Christmas 1999. 'I'll get back to you right after the New Year,' she said.

Sure enough, right after the New Year, the phone rang. But something didn't feel right. The more she talked, the fishier the situation sounded. Finally, I said, 'Look, you've got to be straight with me here because something stinks about this. What's happening here?'

She said, 'It's for David. He wants you to come in. We're going to buy you a plane ticket, just to hang out and meet the guys.'

Immediately, I knew what was up.

'Are you talking about a fucking audition? Because I auditioned in 1974 and I ain't doing it again,' I told her. 'You can tell David that.'

'I'll relay the message,' she said, with a big laugh. 'But no, it's not an audition. You've got the gig.'

I was back in.

In the UK with David to headline Glastonbury Festival in 2000.

13

I'm Baaaaack

By February 2000, I was in a cramped upstairs room on 26th Street in Manhattan, running down tunes with David, guitarist Mark Plati, bassist Gail Ann Dorsey and drummer Sterling Campbell, with an eye on a massive world tour and a headline spot at Glastonbury Festival.

On the first day I was early. As usual, I wanted to get settled and get a feel for the space and the band before things kicked into gear. The rehearsal space was Big Mike's, and we were in a smaller, upstairs studio. It was a cool room, but really, it was too small.

Of course, David wasn't there yet.

Coco Schwab, David's longtime assistant, introduced me to the band, and over the next half-hour we did that introductory thing where everyone's getting a feel for each other. I could tell right away it was a great group of people – and players, of course – and just from the vibe in the room and the sounds we were making while getting in tune, that it was going to work in a big way.

I put on my guitar, just to check my amp out and get settled. We weren't really playing any songs. We were just talking and futzing around. And then David walked in while we were up on the stage.

He looked great. He seemed really healthy, with long hair and dressed fucking cooler than shit. He had a frock coat on. And he had a big smile on his face.

He came up to me right away.

'Well, well, well, I see Mr. Rock and Roll has arrived. Hello, Slicky.'

It was like no time had passed at all. That was the thing about our relationship: from day one, with me coming in and out and in and out for forty goddam years, even when there was some kind of major gap where we absolutely, completely fell out of touch, whenever we saw each other again, it was like we were picking up things the very next day. You can't say that about many people, especially in the music business, but that's the way it was between me and David. There sure wasn't uncomfortableness, like when you haven't seen somebody and you're not sure what to say and all that. None of that. Right away we joked around like old pals. So, the situation was really comfortable and felt good.

I liked the new David Bowie. There was a huge difference in him. When we first worked together, he was totally on another planet and not so pleasant to be around. The same could be said for me, of course. We were both fucked up beyond recognition. By Serious Moonlight, things were a lot better. We all still got high, but for some reason we were able to do it without getting completely stupid. That had been seventeen years ago. In 2000, things looked a lot better.

When David walked into the studio that day, and a big smile crossed his face, I could feel the warmth. I noticed David was a lot softer in a lot of ways. He wasn't as intense.

Sobriety will do that. We talked easily, catching up on what we'd been up to and our respective families.

Pretty soon, everyone was set up, with David in the centre, facing us.

'Right,' he said, 'let's play some songs.' Mark, who'd replaced Carlos as bandleader, kicked things off with the intro lick to 'Stay', but David stopped him immediately. 'No, no. The guy who played it originally is here to play it,' and he pointed at me. 'It's all his.'

I hit the first couple of bars and David's smile got even bigger. He sang the first few lines, then he leaned over and shouted, 'Turn that fucking guitar up!' Off we went. I could tell it was a great band, totally in synch and serving David's songs in the best possible ways. Because all of it was new to me, and because I didn't know any of the players – Mike Garson, the keyboard player, wasn't there yet – I was really keying into everyone and how David was reacting. This band is really fucking good, I thought. 'They're nice people. This will work.'

Afterwards, David and everyone stayed on at the rehearsal place for an hour, and it felt really solid. But after that day we took a break. We didn't play again for almost two months.

After that break, we rehearsed for six weeks for Glaston-bury. Mike Garson, from the Diamond Dogs days, came back on keyboards. I connected from the get-go with Mark Plati, another New Yorker. Plus, Cat Russell – a great musi-cian who could play guitar, keyboards, backing vocals and percussion – had been added. Cat was our 'if nobody else can, she can' player. And we had Gail. The bass player's always the mellow one and she fitted that to a T. And, of course, Sterling on drums.

Mark and Gail and Sterling made an amazing core rhythm section, and all three were great people. Mike Garson played his ass off. We also had Holly Palmer and Emm Gryner, both wonderful solo artists in their own right – which was typical of David, to pick artists who could stand on their own two feet – doing background vocals and percussion. There was no attitude. The band just gelled.

One thing's for sure, 2000 didn't remind me at all of previous times I'd worked with David. It was nothing like '74. Or even '83. The 1974 tour was ambitious, but seat of the pants, and an off-the-rails drug experience, while '83 played to huge stadiums. Not only was this time super organized, with everything First Class, we only had a few gigs, even though one was Glastonbury.

We kicked things off at the Roseland Ballroom in New York City and another show there to 3,000 – pretty small, if you think about it – before heading over to play to almost a million people at Glastonbury.

Glastonbury goes down as one of David's truly great shows, but what stands out to me was Willie Nelson, who went on right before us. Willie was amazing.

Right before we went on, David had a problem that apparently only I could fix. David had only brought one pair of stage shoes, and they didn't fit him right. We wear the same size shoes, which he knew, so right before we went on, he sent Coco to the band's dressing room. 'Slick, David needs your shoes for the show.'

'These are all I've got, Coco,' I told her.

'Well, he'd really appreciate it.'

What was I supposed to wear? 'Fuck it,' I thought. I handed her my boots and put on the Converse sneakers I'd worn with my street clothes before getting on stage to entertain the million good people who'd come to see David, now wearing my boots.

After the show, David kept my boots, but he gave me his shoes, the ones he'd rejected because of the fit. They were stylish and expensive but to me, seemed ugly as hell. Plus, David was right; they didn't fit right. I gave them to a buddy, which I kind of regret.

The rest of the tour was a hodgepodge of shows because it wasn't a full-blown tour. At the end of the tour, we recorded what would become *Toy* as it was known when it was released a few years ago as David's 'lost' album. It was totally last minute and we had no idea we would be making a record. David said offhandedly one day, just after we'd gotten back from playing Glastonbury, 'Oh, by the way, next week we'll be in the studio.' And that was it. No rehearsals, no demos, nothing. He booked Sear Sound – which was the studio that we had recorded *Double Fantasy* in when it had been the Hit Factory – with Mark Plati, essentially, acting as the producer. He played some guitar, too, along with me, Mike Garson, Gail and Sterling, plus Holly and Emm, as the core band. This was the Glaston-bury line-up that also played an amazing show at the BBC Theatre.

For *Toy*, we re-recorded a lot of David's early stuff – early singles and album tracks – that few people, even diehard fans, knew. It was fun and we worked really fast. We weren't given any music to take home to listen to and work on, so whatever happened, happened in the studio. And because we'd been playing a lot, the band was tight and in the same mindset.

The sessions were great. We'd learn the tune with everybody in the room at the same time, including the backing singers – although we'd done a few, like 'I Dig Everything' and 'The London Boys', at gigs like the BBC Radio Theatre show we played after Glastonbury – and then we'd record, completely live. You can even hear it on a tune or two at the end, where you can tell that it's a band playing. You can hear the interaction and everything else that goes on with a bunch of musicians in a room together when a great take is finishing up, and that happened because we had a touring band that went into the studio and was still on it's game as a group. And because of the personalities involved in there, it was super smooth. Plus, David was in a really good mindset – we all were – so we were having a blast.

There were some real stand-out songs, as far as I'm concerned. 'I Dig Everything' is one of my favourites. And 'Shadow Man' is cool, too, as is 'Hole in the Ground' and 'Silly Boy Blue', on which Emm plays clarinet. And I got Mark Plati to employ an old Keith Richards trick, adding two acoustic guitars, so that there'd be one on each side of the stereo spectrum, played ever so slightly differently, to beef up the tracks. He and David loved it. (When *Toy* did eventually come out, in 2022, Mark was able to use those acoustic tracks to make almost a whole alternative version of the album as a really cool bonus disc. So, thanks, Keith!)

After the fact, I went back and listened to some of the songs – whatever was available – and fell in love with David's stuff from long before he ever became famous. It had this cool English R&B edge, like The Small Faces and early Who, combined with a show-tune sensibility, that was strange but amazing, too.

Over a two-week period, at the end of July and into early August of 2000, off and on, it was completely finished. We were on a timer because David's wife, Iman, was pregnant with their daughter and was due. Like clockwork, their daughter Lexi was born right after we finished the sessions.

But then the weirdest thing happened: *Toy* got shelved. We cut an entire album that then just got parcelled out as B-sides and extra songs on Japanese CDs. From that experience, I got really tight with Mark Plati. In between gigs and recording sessions, I wrote songs that Mark was going to produce. The ultimate goal was to try to crack into TV and film scoring, something my mentor Michael Kamen had made a big success of.

After Lexi was born, things got a bit quiet, for obvious reasons. So, Mark and I got down to the serious work of making the album that became *Zig Zag*. One day, I called Mark in the studio. Little did I know David was sitting beside him. When he heard Mark's side of the conversation, he grabbed the phone and said, 'I hear you're recording with Mark. If you need anybody to do tambourines or whatever . . .'

David and I co-wrote 'Isn't It Evening' for the album.

Pretty soon, we also had Def Leppard's Joe Elliott and Robert Smith from The Cure playing on the album.

In return, Robert invited me to play on a new version of 'A Forest'. He asked if I'd be interested in joining The Cure, a gig which, in another twist, went to my old friend Reeves Gabrels, who'd played with David throughout the nineties.

With Reeves and I five years apart in age, by the time I was playing all the places in Staten Island, Reeves, who grew up there, too, was watching my bands play. We didn't know each other, but after I did the Serious Moonlight Tour, Reeves connected with David and Tin Machine happened, with Reeves on guitar. Tin Machine was a whole different thing than I was used to David doing, but I thought it was cool because it was the only time after the Spiders that David had what looked like a real band. I'd gone to see them for that very reason, and I thought they were out there, in a good way, because of the way that Reeves approached the guitar. It definitely sounded better live than on record, which often happened with David. After that, Reeves was off my radar, even though during that period of time Reeves made a lot of records with David and wrote songs with him. It was that period when David went more avant garde, I'm-going-to-purposely-not-write-a-pop-song thing. So, there weren't any 'Fames' or 'Young Americans' or 'Golden Years' or 'Ziggys' to play. None of that. But it wasn't what they were into or trying to achieve.

When Reeves got The Cure gig, I remember my manager at the time, and friends, saying, 'Wow, that really should've been your gig,' and asking, 'Aren't you pissed?' And I said, 'No. No, I'm not.' Because to be honest about the situation, Reeves was probably the better choice out of the two of us for The Cure. We both have our styles and skills, but the things that he's really good at I think slotted right into that gig with Robert and The Cure. I thought Reeves was the better choice for a lot of reasons, and there wasn't any of that professional animosity or whatever you want to call it.

By 2001, with my album *Zig Zag* in the can, I headed to Japan for three months. I knew David was going into the studio, but he'd probably only use me on a few tracks. Even if he used me on the whole album, the difference in the pay to going on the road for three months with a very big Japanese artist was pennies to dollars. I went where the pay cheque was.

I never said anything to David, in fact, but it worked out fine because he had Pete Townshend, The Who's guitarist and an old friend of his, and Gerry Leonard, playing on the album. As it turned out, the songs were more Gerry's cup of tea than mine, so he was the right choice.

Of course, as always with David and his unpredictable nature, in the end I did play a couple of bits here and there, just before the record was finished.

One day, not long after the *Zig Zag* sessions, I was in the city to have lunch with David and I got an unexpected call from Coco.

'David is seriously under the weather, but if you're here anyway, why don't we have lunch?' Coco and I had a great time, talking about old times and what we were both up to. Then, as we were getting up to head our separate ways, she said, 'Hey, let's stop by the studio.'

I didn't know David would be there, but there he was

when we arrived, doing vocals for *Heathen*. I could tell right away when I walked into the studio that he was sick. You could see it. He sounded great, but he just didn't look well. He clearly had some kind of flu or whatever.

When there was a break, David came out, but when I went to shake his hand he said, 'Don't come near me. I'm a germ factory.' We talked from about six feet away from each other, very casual. And in his very typical David Bowie style, he said, 'By the way, what are you doing around April?'

Right away, I knew what was coming next. David was funny like that, and that's why I say it was never malicious when you were 'out' because you'd usually end up back in. A lot of times, it wasn't even premeditated. If you weren't there, and if there was somebody else there, they had a gig because David simply didn't think of you.

I'd showed up without any agenda whatsoever, and almost immediately David asked me to do the Heathen Tour, of course in his typically roundabout way. I found out later that he knew I was coming, but I don't think he'd thought about asking me till I'd walked in the room. When we were talking, it was almost as though I could see his wheels turning. 'Oh God, I love it when Slicky plays. I think I'll have him do this tour.' And to be honest, I didn't care. Not in a 'fuck you, I don't care' kind of way. Everything was cool. I had a record contract. I had – during the course of the gigs we'd done – gotten some press and I was back in the game again. Even though I wasn't all that busy right at that moment, I figured something's going to pop up here somewhere. Don't even worry about it. And then he asked me to do the tour.

I said yes, of course. There was something about our relationship that I knew didn't happen every day. After more than thirty years in the business, I'd learnt that you need to get over yourself and your personal shit and not be thin-skinned. Whatever had happened in 1974, or 1976, or 1983, this was 2000-and-fucking-2. That's a lot of water under the bridge. When you have a creative and professional relationship with somebody that works – because my relationship with David worked, and because whatever went down between us never really had anything to do with my performance or anything like that – you need to cherish and nurture that and let bygones be bygones.

In fact, whatever problems we'd had in the past had always come down to some bullshit business stuff that was most of the time not created by either one of us. There was nothing to get over, really. It was better to just move on. No big deal. It's not as though after work we were hanging out and visiting each other's families and all that bullshit, mind you. But when it came down to the work thing, there was a connection there.

By the time the Heathen Tour came around, there were now two guitar players besides me: Mark Plati and Gerry Leonard. It was a big band. David had also put together a pretty ambitious set list. But I was all in. I had to be. That was the thing. You had to be with David. And that wasn't even a conscious thought, in all honesty. You just had to look at it like, 'Okay, this is where I am right now. Whatever happened before, it doesn't exist anymore. It's gone. And there is no tomorrow yet. So here I am. I want to enjoy this.' So, I knew the score and was all in.

David, meanwhile, looked great. He had a sharp haircut and had chosen some great stage clothes. He seemed in good shape and good voice, too. He'd dropped some of the keys of the songs and, to be honest, some of the songs sounded better in lower keys. He felt young, even though he was pushing sixty.

We had an ambitious rehearsal schedule. Over six weeks of long, focused days, we'd typically start at eleven and finish at about seven at night, with a lunch break of maybe an hour. Maybe.

David got up early in those days. Like, six-in-the-fucking-morning early. So, before rehearsals at eleven, he would be doing press for the tour, photo sessions, whatever. And then he would come to rehearsal and we would work the whole time he was there.

He was hands-on, which was something he hadn't been in the past. It was a different band, of course – but by no means was it any less of a band – and as good as the 2000 band, which I thought had been one of David's best. But it was a different band.

One thing that we did – and everybody used to do it, though you don't see it as much anymore – was focus on the new material from the new album. Nowadays, with the exception of a few pop stars, most of the acts that are out on the road filling arenas and stadiums are not twenty-five years old. The market isn't there. It doesn't exist. There's no such thing as a young David Bowie or Elvis or Beatles or Stones. Those sorts of artists are gone. History. All the old motherfuckers that are out there doing it are playing greatest hits. Almost no new artists have come along with that level of talent, who make great music and have the sort of rabid following that those acts enjoyed back in the day. Again, there are exceptions, so don't fight me.

But when we went out on tour, David was still doing it the old-school way. He'd make a record and the tour would be about that record. That would be the focus, even though we would be playing all the other material – 'Rebel', 'Let's Dance', 'Diamond Dogs' and all the Ziggy stuff – the focus would be on *Heathen*. It was called the Heathen Tour, and we played just about the whole record throughout the show, though of course not all in a row. That was how you did things up until about that time. If you had a new record out and you were touring, you had to play those songs if you wanted to sell records.

It worked. That record did sell. That's when the internet was just hitting full fucking swing, going from the old era to the new one, like a lightning bolt. By the time we finished *Reality*, just two years later, we found ourselves in a completely different world.

After thirty-six dates over four months across Europe and North America, David only took two months off before getting the band back into the studio to record *Reality* with Tony Visconti producing.

There wasn't a pause between Heathen and Reality. It was like one long, never-ending tour. When we finished the Heathen Tour, David said, 'You know what, guys? This is just a break, a rest. We're not taking off a lot of time. You know what we're doing next? We're making another record and we're going back out and, next time, we're going to go out longer.' So, it was continuous. Even as we got towards the last quarter of the Reality Tour, David already had a plan in place for what was going to happen, starting in 2005, in the post-Reality Tour era.

At that point, David knew himself really well, as most of us do by the time we reach middle age. He knew damn well that if we finished off without a plan, and he wasn't diligent about what would happen next, even in his own mind, then we'd end up in a Twilight Zone of two, three, maybe even five years, not really doing anything. He just kept it rolling; number one, because we were making a lot of money, but mainly, I think, because he was enjoying himself. We did a lot of cool things that he hadn't done in a while. We appeared on every American TV show you could do and, in the UK, we did a shitload of primetime TV, like *Jonathan Ross*. Similarly, in France, Germany and Italy, it was one thing after the next. I barely remember any of it unless something comes up on YouTube or my social media, there was so much promo. Shit pops up that I've completely forgotten about because if you cram that much into such a small space of time, you're not going to remember everything.

The point is we never, in the past, operated on that paradigm. Ever. Back in the old days, it was all very seat of the pants. Now, there was something approaching a masterplan.

In the spring of 2004, before we finished the Reality Tour, David and I had a long conversation about his plans. We were sitting in a makeshift dressing room in a trailer at an outdoor gig where the Stereophonics opened for us. David came in and grabbed me and Gerry and said, 'Look, guys, we're going to finish up in a few months. I'm not going out for a year at a time anymore. What I want to do at this point is what will be fun, and make sense for you guys and for me, is to do three months a year for the next four or five years of records. That way, we could do Radio City Music Hall for a week, then we could go to Chicago and do a week there, then we'd go to LA and do the Shrine Auditorium for a week. It won't be a one-nighter or a two-nighter. It'll be a whole week. We'll get where we're going, check into our hotel, do our gigs every day, for a week, and move on. In three months, we'll be done. That way, we can rehearse for a month, go out, do three months, and the rest of the year is yours to do whatever you want with.'

I loved it. I thought, 'Fuck, this is perfect. It makes so much sense. Now I'll have got three months of pay, which will more than take care of me for quite a while, and then I'll have eight months off, with a shitload of press from the gigs, and money in my pocket.' That meant I could pursue other stuff, but I wouldn't have to be squeezing it in, during whatever brief downtime I might have from working with David. I'd actually have a nice chunk of time to do whatever cool shit might come my way, without hurting my relationship with David, because it would be just normal work during a gap between tours.

It was like the best of both worlds. I'd have the visibility of working with David, but also people would know when I was off the road because it would be extremely obvious, and knowing the way David does his press, he would've explained it all in his interviews. The fans would be saying, 'Hey, this is fucking cool. Bowie's going to be touring for a

while, and I get to see him once a year in a cool theatre setting.' And from my point of view, it would look to people
who might want to work with me like, 'He just finished
David's tour, so it looks like he's free for a while.' The visibility would give me a hell of an advantage because I
wouldn't be disappearing, and at the same time folks in the
business would know when I was going to be available to
work, and anyone else wanting to work with me would
know that, too.

At the same time, it would just be a gap. Albeit a long gap,
but a gap. Not an end. That was going to be a big difference,
psychologically, for the audience, and for the band, too. It
wasn't going to be like the old days, where you'd finish up a
tour and you'd think to yourself, 'What am I going to do
now?' Because David never really said much in the old days
about what was going to happen next, usually because he
didn't know.

At the time we were on the road with *Heathen* and making
Reality, and then touring that record, David was in really
good shape, whatever you might have read or heard. He
looked good. He was singing really great. I liked the work
we were doing, too. I like *Reality* a lot.

The sessions for *Reality* were different, mind you. After
we did *Toy*, which we recorded as a band album, working on
old songs that David wanted to revisit, now it was 2003 and
David was writing as we went along. That was something
he'd always done. It was nothing new. He'd never walk in
with a whole record finished. But what was different was
that we recorded that album as overdubs, with each person
recording their specific parts individually, one at a time. The

only things we recorded as a band during that period of time were a reworking of 'Rebel' for the soundtrack to one of the *Charlie's Angels* films, and a recording of the Kinks classic 'Waterloo Sunset'. Those were recorded as a band, though it wasn't the whole band. It was recorded with just me, Sterling, Gerry and Tony Visconti, the producer, playing bass. Other than that, the record was parted out, and done in chunks.

The office would call me, and I'd troop down to the studio. David and Tony would play me whatever rhythm tracks or partial tracks they had down, and I would put my parts on. That's the first time I'd made a record like that with David. I thought that was a shame, because the band was really great by that time after playing together for a few years. But the band was never in the studio together in its entirety to record.

Mark Plati, at that point, was still with us. This was before the tour, so Mark was still in. In fact, I hadn't heard anything about Mark leaving the band until it happened, just before the tour. Mark played bass and guitar and he played a lot on *Reality* and had a big role, even though Tony Visconti was the producer. But I think, in the end, that might have been the problem. Mark had been David's producer, mixer, musical director and all-around studio hand for about six years at that point. All of a sudden, out of nowhere, Tony Visconti, who had disappeared for a while, re-entered the picture. It definitely caused problems. It didn't matter that it was Tony, mind you. It wouldn't have mattered who it was showing up. When you have a gig like that, and all of a sudden someone just sort of materializes out of thin air and you're out of a gig – or at least your main gig, as producer – it's the beginning of the end.

I loved Mark, and I felt terrible for him, but also, it was his first taste of that part of David, whereas I'd already been through that shit many, many times. So many times, in fact, that I didn't even think about it anymore. To me, it was business as usual. 'David doesn't know what he wants to do, so I might be out of here. I could be working at a fucking car wash tomorrow for all I know.'

Mark had never experienced that before.

At the beginning of the tour, we filmed our show in Dublin for what would become the *A Reality Tour* DVD and concert film. It was ridiculous, but they always do that; record and film a show before the kinks are all worked out. Almost every live record or DVD I've ever done in my life on a big tour came from the beginning of the run. It's self-defeating because the band hasn't gotten on a roll yet. It sure wasn't David's idea. It was, as usual, the fucking record company pushing that genius move. So, we recorded that show in November of 2003, after we'd only been out on the road for a short time, when we should have waited till we had half the tour under our belts and were really killing it.

Obviously, I was disappointed in the way it turned out. I know fans love that DVD, and David and the band did look great and played a really solid show, but a lot of it had to do with the way it sounded. I didn't like the way the show sounded on the DVD or the record. I thought we lost a lot of our oomph. The guy that recorded and produced the original recordings – because that performance was reissued and reissued, with differing credits for each release – didn't do us justice. The band sounded a lot smaller than our impact live, whereas on the *David Live* album it sounded just like the band did live.

People always ask me what my favourite songs to play live with David were. To be honest, from my vantage point, I was always watching what was going on on stage more than I was what was going on in the audience because I was focused on the songs and the band. Sure, an audience feeds you, but what really feeds me is the interaction within the band. There'd always be little key things I'd watch for, probably from Sterling more than anybody else, because I always feed off the drummer. That's my main thing. The way he played drums and the way I play guitar were a good match, especially because our off-stage relationship is really close. I love Sterling. And we had that 'thing' onstage as a result. But there'd be certain parts of the show where I'd zero in on Gail or Gerry or David, because that's where my energy surge comes from. As a result, my favourite songs would change constantly.

I always liked playing 'Heroes', though, and I always liked playing 'Diamond Dogs'. But for a song like 'Rebel', I would have to hold my nose through it, mainly because I'd played it way too many times. I really got into 'Fame', though, because I figured out that I could weave in and out of whatever Carlos or Plati or Gerry were doing. And I liked playing 'The Man Who Sold the World' and I used to really like playing 'Queen Bitch', though David didn't do that one much. But sometimes my favourite song would be my favourite song until we played it too many times. And then it became, 'Oh no, not that one again!'

I also liked playing the title track from *Reality*. And I liked playing '5:15' and the title track to *Heathen*. There was a lot of cool stuff on those records that I really enjoyed playing live. But because I had a lot to do with the making of *Reality*, those songs always felt really great. When I've played songs on a record and we would then do them in concert, they'd come to mean something different in the live setting, so I'd tend to be more excited about playing them over something I had little or nothing to do with.

There were some oddball favourites, too, even if we didn't do them all that often. I remember doing 'The Motel' at Madison Square Garden, and that didn't go down too well. Within the first twenty-five seconds of the song, you could see the audience getting up to go get popcorn. Even though when we did it in Europe they were running to the stage, you don't do a song like that in New York City, where all they want to hear is 'Let's Dance', 'Rebel', 'China Girl' and the other ones I'm sure David felt he'd beaten to death. Even if we'd done 'Word on a Wing' off *Station*, they would've gone and got popcorn. If he'd done 'Stay', of course, they'd be fine. 'Golden Years'? Okay. 'The Motel', and it was popcorn time.

The rest of the shows on that tour went great. We criss-crossed the world, and David was having a blast.

On that tour, we used a private company and we all travelled together. It wasn't like the tricked-out plane we had on the Serious Moonlight Tour, which was a 707 jumbo jet that had been completely converted, with living rooms and bedrooms and TV rooms and even fucking staff. That was insane. This wasn't like that. We had a turboprop plane because they have the best safety record. It was just a regular turboprop with regular seats in it. Nothing special. David got it for safety reasons, but the funny thing is, after all that, it backfired because a turboprop cannot fly at 36,000 feet, which you want to do to avoid bad weather and clouds and turbulence. Since turboprops can't go that high, we rode either right above or right below the weather. Every fucking flight we took was like a roller coaster. And David didn't like to fly. On one hand, logically, he felt safe. But watching him sit there while we were going through these storms and shit was terrible.

David didn't talk about his family that much, except for his new baby, Alexandria – or Lexi, as we came to think of her – the new kid on the block. She was only a few years old. It wasn't that he'd get into big conversations about her, he'd just mention, 'Oh, yeah, my little girl just did the most wonderful thing . . .' the way that dads do. We did see Iman, and even Lexi, a few times when we were in the New York area, but that was it. That wasn't unusual. You don't really spend a whole lot of time talking about your home life or family when you're working like that, and if you started doing it when you were young, this automatic shutdown happens when you leave home. 'Now, I'm on the road.' That's what you're doing and that's who you *are*. You can't bring home on the road with you. I've seen guys do it. They're miserable. I always loved being on the road – and still do – and have no problem separating home from work. I don't even consciously do it, nor have I ever really thought much about it, but I tune everything out. That's why it's very easy for me. I'm in 'road mode'. Period.

Meanwhile, David was performing great, and I could tell that he was really enjoying himself. He was in great spirits, and everything was rolling along better than ever. When he took sick, as the tour wound down, it was a real surprise because you wouldn't have thought it. When you think of people having anything like a heart problem, or something like that, you think, number one, they're over-weight or don't look good. But he looked great, he was singing great. His energy level was fucking great. And then, all of a sudden, he started not looking so good for about a week or two. And then that was it.

We were blind-sided because everything seemed fine. David was fine. One minute he was talking about what he wanted to do next because we were getting towards the end of the tour, and then, all of a sudden, out of nowhere, he wasn't looking good and was complaining about how he was feeling. It was just that fast. It didn't happen over a month or two. It was literally over a couple of weeks, if that.

We all watched it happening. There was the incident in Prague, of course, where he apparently had a mild heart attack. I don't know if you'd want to call it mild because a heart attack's a heart attack. I was onstage with him when it happened, and you could see up close that things were not good. He was helped off the stage, but then he came back out again, for some reason. But he only lasted about a half a song, and that was it. He was gone.

After that, we cancelled a few gigs, but pretty soon we

were back out on the road and played the Hurricane Festival in Germany. And that's when I knew that it was over. First of all, the weather was really shitty. June in Germany is gloomy and cold and rainy, and that night was all three. We were doing this outdoor gig, there was mud everywhere and the dressing rooms were shitty little tents. Before the show, David was sitting in the corner, looking like he was freezing, and green to the gills. But it wasn't the weather. You could see that. I knew something was really wrong.

The weird thing was, as crappy as he looked before the show, once he got onstage, he kicked ass. It was another typical David moment, after a lifetime together of moments like that, where he'd pull magic out of the hat. But that was it. That was the last gig we did. Ever.

Top: Backstage with David signing merch. *Bottom:* The early days of the Slick Strap company, which led to Slick Guitars.

14

Without David

David went straight from the Hurricane Festival stage in Hamburg into surgery, but nobody said anything to us. We headed back to Hamburg, and I remember being there for three or four days, hanging out, going out for dinners and whatever, and wondering what the hell was happening, but also knowing what the silence meant.

They cancelled a few more gigs, so amongst the band we figured maybe David's team was waiting to see how he was feeling. That wasn't the case. During that gap of a few days, David's team were tying up loose ends, figuring out how to get everybody home.

Of course, when we all landed, and headed our separate ways, it was pretty obvious what was going on. I went about my business. I certainly didn't sit by the phone or anything because by that point, on a subconscious level more than anything, the writing was on the wall.

The band was pretty tight by that time, so we talked back and forth, but there wasn't really a whole lot to say. We were all in 'what the fuck's going on?' mode. None of us knew anything. Whatever there was to talk about wasn't mentioned, because it was too depressing to face the unspoken question, 'Was David going to die?' No one was going there. I would remember it if they had.

When I got back, my house was undergoing a full renovation. After being on the road for a year and actually not even feeling burned out – I probably felt more energetic and healthier when I got home than before I left – I went about my business. I took on overseeing the construction they were doing at the house, staying in a nice resort nearby while the work was being done. I had all the time I wanted for myself because every day at that point I had been scheduled to be out on the road with David. I really didn't do a whole lot of anything. And there really was no reason to.

So that was that. Slowly, I started getting curious. Of course, I wasn't going to get any answers from David's office. I'd called once, twice . . . nothing.

Then, suddenly, there were rumblings from David's office about going out again. I was already busy testing the waters, looking to find somebody who might be on the hunt for a guitar player, and I had spoken to a few people. I had one gig pretty much in the bag, and then, out of nowhere – and nobody even called me about it – there was a fucking press announcement.

'David Bowie to Tour!'

The band members' names were all there, including mine. The people I'd been negotiating for work with saw that, and the negotiations stopped. They said, 'We see what's going on in the press here and, as far as we can tell, your allegiance is with Bowie. We can't take a chance on bringing you on, and you taking off.'

Once again. It cost me dearly. It really did. Because how

can you convince somebody to ignore what they're seeing with their own eyes? You can't. If you're on their end of the stick, you're thinking, 'This guy could tell us anything he fucking wants to. He could say that he wants to work with us because he's unsure if David's even going out. But if David really pushes the button, what is he going to do? He's going with David and he's going to leave us high and dry.' That's what they're thinking. And they're right to think it. You can't get around that.

That happened again a few more times over the next couple of years. David's office would call me and put me on hold. The next time was at the beginning of 2006. 'Yup, we're thinking of doing something. We're giving you some notice here, and we'll let you know as soon as we're ready to go.'

It never happened, of course.

In the meantime, work opportunities continued to come up here and there. I played with Buddy Guy. I was invited to play alongside Chuck Berry in a tribute gig organized by the Rock and Roll Hall of Fame, followed a year later with a tribute to The Rolling Stones playing with the likes of Nils Lofgren, Bobby Keys, Steve Jordan and a whole host of Stones alumni.

The Slick gear thing – my own line of artist model guitars, straps and all that – started around that same time, in 2008, and really took off, even though there was no intent behind it. It started out really simply. I had some road cases around the house from the last Bowie tour that hadn't been opened since they'd been shipped back to me in 2004. There was one utility case in and amongst the guitar cases and amplifier cases, and I opened it up and found at least half a dozen black leather guitar straps. I thought, 'What am I going to do with these things?' And, for some reason, I thought, 'What if I distress these – get a sander or something – and see what they look like?' One thing led to another, and I eventually used some stencils I had laying around to do artwork on them once they were distressed to my liking, and I was really happy with the way they turned out. I brought them to Jay Abend, the owner of guitarfetish.com, a great guy I'd met in the 1980s in the midst of my insane, drugged-out days. He had been my artist representative at Guild Guitars, whose acoustics around that time were really on the money. So, Jay and I go back that far, and we'd stayed in touch because I'd run into him at NAMM over the years. In the meantime, he'd set up the Guitar Fetish business. So, I visited Jay at his house in Massachusetts and when I walked in, I threw a bunch of the straps on his kitchen table. He freaked out. 'What are those? We've got to put these in our product line!'

For the next three or four months, I worked really hard, six days a week, making prototypes. In fact, Steve Lukather got one of the first straps, a prototype with turquoise skulls on it, that he still uses. But I made hundreds of them, and then we picked out the ones that he thought would sell best on the site.

Eventually, we developed Slick Guitars, too, an extremely reasonably priced guitar that plays and sounds great. And we have Slick pickups, too. There's a whole line of Slick gear now, which has been great because between the business changing and the pandemic – not to mention that lots of the big artists who used to call aren't around anymore, and those sidemen gigs, with the Bowies of the world, just don't exist – it's been a great creative outlet for me, as well as a nice source of income. So, guitarfetish.com has turned out to be my retirement plan, just like the normies have. A decade-plus down the line, I'm drawing an income off it every month. It's worked out really well.

Otherwise, the rest of the decade was a scramble. Let's just call it what it was: the damage that was done to my career – the perception within the industry that I was unavailable via my relationship with David Bowie – really threw a wrench in the works. Me and some of the guys that had been around with David longer called it the 'Bowie curse'. Because you were looked at as one of 'Bowie's guys'.

Being known as one of Bowie's guys sure didn't put off David Johansen, though. When The New York Dolls needed a lead guitarist for a new album they were recording and a tour they had planned for 2011, my phone rang. Johansen and I went way back, so I said yes right away, and we had a blast, travelling all over, playing Dolls classics and some of the band's really excellent new material. In fact, as soon as the press hit that I was doing it, the other David in my life – David Bowie – called. 'You're going to record with Johansen? That's fucking cool, man. Congratulations. Have a great time. I'm real happy for you.'

I never gave up on David – I'd get emails on my birthday, Christmas and so forth – but after all the false alarms a few years earlier, I'd just stopped expecting anything.

Then I went out in a friend's gorgeous custom-built Shelby Cobra. On a quiet residential street in Montclair,

New Jersey, it bucked a bit. The motherfucker burst into flames with me behind the wheel.

Pretty soon the internet lit up with reports of a fireball featuring David Bowie's guitar player. It didn't take long for the boss to notice.

'You okay?' he emailed. Two hours later, another message came in, 'What are you up to?' The emails went to and fro for the rest of the day. He kept picking my brain, so I knew it was going somewhere.

'You got something on your mind?' I asked finally.

'Yeah, I'm in the studio making a record and I really want you to play on a couple of tracks. But you need to shut up. Don't talk to anybody about this.'

Top: Trading licks with blues legend Buddy Guy.
Bottom: On stage with The New York Dolls in 2011.

The Next Day and Beyond

When I arrived at the Magic Shop, the first thing I noticed was David's age. It had been almost ten years since I'd seen him. He looked healthy, with a clear-eyed intensity and focus that I didn't recall from the days when everything around us was going a million miles an hour. He looked as though he'd been working hard, which had never really shown on him, so at first, he didn't feel like the guy I'd known for so many years. It wasn't as though David seemed ill or anything like that. He just seemed like a guy with a lot on his plate who, like a lot of artists nowadays have to do, was basically managing himself, raising a family and trying to create, all at the same time.

David introduced me to Mario McNulty, his engineer, who ironically was already one of my best pals in the business. Tony Visconti was there, of course, helping David produce the record, and Sterling Campbell was there, too. It looked like we were going to set up as a live band to record a few tracks. Meanwhile, Coco was popping in and out to see if David needed anything.

Nobody was there who didn't need to be there. The sessions were top secret but recording sessions devoid of any hangers on weren't unusual for David, who liked it that

way. Things were focused and lean, unlike the party atmosphere of some of the other folks I've worked with.

The control room of the Magic Shop had a huge, wrap-
around mixing console and a big comfortable control
room where everyone congregated. Once I'd gotten the
lay of the land, I headed into the live room, where my guitars and amp were already set up.

I was surprised to find that the live room was pretty
down and dirty. The studio where we cut the amazing-
sounding tracks on *The Next Day* looked little more than a
rehearsal space – no frills, carpeted and with Sterling's
drums way at the back of the room, far away from where
the rest of us were set up – but it sure got the job done.

The record was pretty much finished when I got there,
and so my first day in the studio was supposed to mark the
end of tracking, though David ended up taking a break
and finished the vocals up later.

The best part of the experience was that we recorded
three songs live. There was 'Valentine's Day', and '(You
Will) Set the World on Fire', which we actually re-recorded
because David said he hadn't had the right combination of
people he needed to cut it the way he wanted on the first
go round. In fact, the song was memorable because it was
100 per cent finished. The lyrics were done – everything
was done – which was never the way David worked. But
he told me that he hadn't found the song he had in his
head yet, and that I was the lynchpin to get that one done.
We also recorded 'Dirty Boys', a song that felt like something David really hadn't done before, but still touched on
elements of things from his past.

For the three songs we cut live, we didn't nitpick. We knocked around some ideas, and we got it done. As soon as it felt good, Tony would hit record. I also overdubbed some parts on another five tracks that were already done but needed a lead guitar. On those, they had Gerry Leonard's atmospheric stuff, but they needed some of my crunch. So, we got a lot of work done in a short period of time; just five days in all.

Meanwhile, on that first day, we got down to work and really quickly, with lots of smiles, we had the take he had in mind.

As for 'Valentine's Day', he had just finished writing that one, so he was still tinkering around with bits and pieces here and there while we were in the studio, messing around with the arrangement.

Suddenly, he decided he wanted to give it a go. We discussed what he'd come up with, and we went through the arrangement ideas we all had – with me on guitar, Sterling Campbell on drums, Tony Visconti on bass and David singing – and he finished rewriting based on that, right there and then, and we cut it.

I remember wondering why Sterling was there when I arrived. In hindsight, I realized that David had already decided that he wanted to cut those two songs live. Of course, they were two completely different types of songs, so it was cool doing them all together in a room live. With 'Set the World on Fire', basically any time we spent on it before we actually pressed the old record button was just tidying it up. 'Valentine's Day', however, was more of an open canvas. There was a bridge that ended up getting cut, and the whole vibe of the song was what was put together in the studio because David had written it on an acoustic guitar and that's all he had.

While David had been playing with the lyrics, Tony had showed me the parts because he had a rough demo of the song, and I kind of took those parts and played them the way I would play them.

Plus, they didn't have the riff that drives the song, which we came up with the way we did a lot of other stuff: David had his chord changes, and the basic structure of the song, along with a basic melody and maybe some of the lyrics. I got a feel for where he was going and what he was trying to do, and when he played it to me, because of the melody, the lyrics and those chord changes, I got ideas, instantly.

This feels like The Kinks, I kept thinking, because if you listen to the basic track of 'Valentine's Day' you can hear licks that sound sonically similar to 'Waterloo Sunset', The Kinks' signature song, filled with the sort of guitar parts that Dave Davies made famous and that I have made my stock and trade.

I said to David, 'Kinks. "Waterloo".'

He said, 'Fuck yeah!'

That's the road we went down, and once we got the basic tracks down, in just two or three takes, the overdubs – the melodies and bits and pieces of guitar, like the opening riff and some of the other riffs in there – came together really quickly. We kept going over and over the track, filling in where he wanted riffs, in his usual way.

It was David's typical way of working.

'You got any ideas?'

'Well, I've got this and this.'

'Well, that's cool, and I've got one for the next part.'

He'd give me a rough idea of what he wanted, and I would take that and Slickify it. Just like the old days, we had enough ideas once we put our heads together to come up with what he needed to finish the track and put it over the top.

Within a few hours we completed both songs.

One thing that needs to be clear is that every record of David's that I know anything about – including the ones that I didn't work on – is truly a David Bowie record. The only record that I could say definitively, just by hearing it, that it wasn't 100 per cent David was *Let's Dance*. Even though I wasn't there, I didn't have to be there. You can hear so much of producer Nile Rodgers' influence on every song on that one that it really is almost like his record with David singing, and unlike any other Bowie record ever recorded. To me, it's almost a Nile Rodgers/David Bowie record.

The Next Day was not like that. When I worked with him, David approached things in a very particular way, totally hands-on, every fucking minute for everything that was going on. He didn't phone things in – then or ever – and never did anything like go out for a walk, saying, 'Put a solo on that, see you later.' He was right there every step of the way because he knew what he wanted, and one of the best talents that man had was picking the right guy for the right job and helping them achieve exactly what he envisioned.

That also explains periods when some of us were in and out, or just disappeared into thin air, over the years. When you're making a record with songs like 'Scary Monsters' and 'Heroes' on them, you're not calling me. There's really no reason to have me there. You're calling Adrian Belew and you're calling Robert Fripp for those kinds of songs. But on something like *The Next Day*, where there were a number of songs on the record that really needed a certain type of playing, I'm the guy you call. No disrespect to Gerry Leonard or David Torn, who also played on the record, and are amazing, formidable players in their own right, but they can't do what I do.

At the end of the day, it was David running the show, hands-on. Very involved. And also, because of him being that hands-on, and just the two of us being the only people in there, along with Tony Visconti, it gave me more leeway to throw my ideas at him and work things out in a more balanced way. There were no distractions because the old adage about too many cooks spoiling the supper is absolutely true. All of a sudden, this guy's got that idea, that guitarist has an idea. We didn't have to deal with any of that. When we did those overdubs – like on *Station to Station* – it was just, 'Okay, we got Slicky in here. Let's make the best use of him in the time we've got him.' That's exactly how it was, and the proof's in the pudding. You can hear it.

Meanwhile, that was the one time I really couldn't read David that well as far as what his plans were for once the record came out. I thought I could, and I thought I was reading him pretty well after we cut one of the tunes, 'Set the World on Fire', which is such a rocker and really sounded killer and energetic, and he said, 'Man, that would be great live.' I looked at him, and I was about to open my mouth, but he said, 'Don't even think about it.'

David was not going out again. I could see it in his eyes. In fact, that's when I started figuring out that there was something happening, not in terms of any illness, but that he had hit a wall about going out again. Because he caught himself.

He'd gotten so excited by the track that his head went right to the stage. But then he nipped it right there. He stopped the idea in its tracks before either of us could say another word.

When we wrapped at the studio on the final day, he was so out of there. It was the last day of recording – except for finishing his vocals – and it felt as though he was gone practically from the minute he walked in, which was really unusual. He'd come in late, we didn't do a whole lot of work because we'd finished the bulk of what he'd wanted to get done in the first four days, and he seemed distracted.

On that last day, his staff were closing and tidying everything up, organizing all his stuff. Whatever guitars he had around, notebooks, were all being packed up to be delivered back to his house, and I could see that was what he was preoccupied with. He was going home. He only lived three blocks away from the studio, but still, he was done. And that's when I looked at him and thought, I've never seen him this antsy to just finish something and fucking leave. Oddly enough, something told me he was more than just done for that day. In the back of my mind, I remember thinking, 'I don't think we're going to see the light of day again.' And I was right, although it was something I'd forgotten about until a couple of years after the fact.

After David died, I started to glue some things together. Because, in all reality, there was an inkling of him not being well at the time. But like anybody, he wasn't one to be spilling that on everybody. If there were things going on with him, there was no way that I would be privy to that information. David was extremely private. He wasn't going to talk about it. That just wasn't David's deal.

On 'Valentine's Day', for the main little melody lead line – though not the solos – David had this little box, not much bigger than a pack of cigarettes. I don't know what it was, but it was this cheesy little thing you were supposed to plug your guitar into to connect it to your computer. David had found the sound he wanted for the song by experimenting with it, so we plugged it into my amp, and it sounded cool. David was really good at that kind of thing; to get something unique. It was usually something pretty simple, but maybe not so obvious.

During those sessions for *The Next Day*, we were older, obviously, and there was no dope. None. In 2000 we had both been clean, so by 2012 we had long time sobriety. It wasn't even a part of our lives anymore. But what we were doing then was we were hammering espresso.

The habit had started when we did *Reality*. We were staying at the Southgate Hotel and on the weekends – the rehearsals for all those tours in the 2000s, except the first few weeks, had pretty regular work hours, with weekends off – I loved taking walks down to Little Italy and China-town. At a great bakery that's been there forever called Bella Ferrara, a little, old-school place, I'd pick up biscotti, which are insanely good, and bring them to the rehearsals.

David would smash a whole box of them. He'd kill them. Along with his espresso, of course.

When we got to *The Next Day*, on my first day there I stopped at the bakery on the way and I picked up a box of those biscotti. David picked up pastries from Dean & DeLuca, and we had an espresso machine in the studio, and we just hammered the shit out of all of it, just like we had fifteen years before. The Magic Shop had a very big control room, and we made ourselves at home and were like pigs in shit. In the old days, we would have done the same thing, only with different substances. We'd sit in the control room and blow our brains out and not start working till hours later. Many hours. Sometimes days later. But this time around, we sat there and hammered espresso and ate biscotti and pastries while we learnt the songs. The routine didn't change, just the substances. And I didn't have to go to rehab after we finished that record.

The single 'Where Are We Now?' was a surprise release on David's birthday, 8 January, in 2013 and then the album came out, to fantastic acclaim. David disappeared again. It was a great magic act in this 24/7 internet age to keep something that big a secret until it became available to the public. I don't know of anyone else who could have pulled that off, to be honest.

Meanwhile, the press scrambled for any tidbit of information. Tony did some press, and I did a little bit, too, taking whatever interviews were thrown my way. I wasn't wary of doing press because it wasn't like the old days, where we would make a record and were getting ready to do a tour, and I'd be doing phone interviews every day for weeks, even into rehearsals and during the tour. That wasn't the case this time around, for obvious reasons. There was the odd interview here and there, but in all, if I did ten interviews, that was a lot.

I didn't feel wary anymore. I was forever 'David Bowie's guitar player'. It was that way long before *The Next Day* came along, so why not take the gig or agree to the interviews? It couldn't do any more damage at that point. I don't use the word 'damage' in a negative sense. As I've said, it just came with the territory and I'd long since come to terms with it. You can call it collateral damage, I guess. Nothing was ever ill-intended. It just happened. It was just something that you needed to be aware of and be able to digest and deal with without turning yourself upside down. Because, if you think about it, it's not insignificant. It's my career, it's my livelihood, it pays my bills, and it's what allows me to play great music with great people, and it's always on the verge of either being taken away or imploding. That weighs on my subconscious. It really does. And that's a point that I don't think most people understand, and maybe even I don't understand, even though I've been through it enough times that I should understand what's happening.

In the aftermath of the release of *The Next Day*, I knew I would not be working with David again. I just did. It wasn't on an intellectual level, though. And it wasn't hearsay coming from his office. It was from what I'd seen with my own two eyes. I'd spent a week with the guy, and I could see and feel where he was at. Plus, there weren't any false starts about touring or anything after that, as there had been after his heart attack. That was it. It was kind of, 'Well, that's that.' Even when there were rumours of a pay-per-view simulcast mini-tour, I was absolutely certain it wasn't happening.

Over the years, the only contact I had with David was the normal contact you might have with someone you'd known and worked with for a long time. The last time I heard from him was on my birthday, in October 2015. The phone rang, and I picked it up.

'Hey, Slicky. I just wanted to make sure I wished you a happy birthday. I sent the email, but I figured I'd give you a quick call. You alright?'

'Yeah, how you doing, boss?'

'Cool.'

That was it, in essence. Of course, it wasn't that abrupt, but that was it beyond some personal chat that I'll keep between the two of us. But he sure didn't get into anything that was going on with his health.

'Hey, man, thanks for calling. Goodbye.'

And with that, David Bowie, the man I'd known since we were practically kids, was gone from my life.

Brian Eno portrayed their email exchanges after David's passing as his way of saying goodbye. But I didn't pick up on that. In retrospect, of course, why else, after forty years, would the guy call me for my birthday? Maybe he had meant to say more. Or maybe he just needed to, for lack of a better way of saying it, put things to bed with me. In other words, 'I'm out of here soon. For whatever it's worth, I'd like to hear some voices of the people I've had in my life for a really long time.' That feels like him. It could've been that. Or maybe, like Brian, he was giving me a little bit of a goodbye. I don't know. But the call was not made without a reason.

How did I find out David Bowie had died? The internet.

It was really weird, too, because he wasn't on my radar at the time, and I wasn't putting much thought into what he was doing or not doing. I didn't even realize he was sick or had an album coming out and a musical on Off-Broadway. Of course, it wasn't the first time we'd gone a long period without anything happening between us, but when I think about it, the time between making *The Next Day* and finding out he'd died kind of flew by.

On the night it happened, my girlfriend at the time was on her phone when she looked at me, ashen, and said, 'I've got something here. Let me sit down. I've got to double-check this.' Then she told me what happened.

It felt weird, because even though we hadn't seen a lot of each other for quite a while, the shock of it – and finding out that way – was surreal. I hadn't seen him for three and a half years at that point, so it really was almost . . . not real. In fact, I hadn't seen the guy but four or five times over the last ten years, but he was still so present in my life, nearly every day, because of the impact the relationship had had on me from the time I started working with him at twenty-three years old in 1974. So yeah, it was a really weird feeling.

The best thing that happened after the fact was when, within a month, British TV contacted the band because David was getting a lifetime achievement award at the Brit

Awards. They wanted the band to perform before the award was presented. That really helped because the band obviously hadn't been playing together and we lived all over the place, so there was an opportunity for us to be together. That helped to put whatever feelings of loss or grief I was having to bed. It put it into perspective. Because for a long time, it just didn't seem real. Being with the band at the Brits, without David there in the middle of us, *that* made it real, and gave it closure, for all of us, I think.

After David died, I didn't pick the phone up for the most part. I just talked to two or three people – maybe – within the couple of days following what happened because less than an hour after the news of his death hit the press, my phone started ringing. It was three o'clock in the morning in New York, but one after the other, they were calling. Eventually, I just pulled the phone out of the wall because I knew what was coming and I really didn't need that shit right at that moment.

I checked my messages the next day because I wanted to make sure there wasn't anybody who was a real friend and really cared who had called. Those I wrote down and made a note to call them when I was up for it. But most of them were this news outlet, that magazine, TV people, radio people, you fucking name it. That was mostly who had called. As I knew it would be.

The first couple of phone calls that came in I did pick up. The first one was my good friend Vernon Reid, the guitar player from the band Living Colour. I only picked it up because I saw his name on the caller ID. He was great, and comforting. Sterling Campbell called, but that might've been everyone I talked to that night. After that I thought, 'I don't need to be talking about this to anyone else right now.' That was it. I unplugged the phone.

It was obviously different from losing someone you see every single day. It was almost as though David wasn't even a real person, in that sense, because we'd spent a lot of time together, in really intimate settings, and he'd departed the planet, but I hadn't seen him all that much recently, so nothing was different. Nothing in my life had changed except that I knew for sure we were definitely not doing anything anymore. It's done. You're not seeing him anymore. He's not here. That might sound kind of callous, but it helped put everything into perspective and put it to bed. It really did. There were a lot of moments where I'd have to catch myself with a sharp reminder that I wouldn't be seeing him anymore, no more finding the right riff to finish a song or seeing his big welcoming smile after a long absence.

Working with David was my first big gig. Talk about going from being obscure to internationally recognizable in a day because of your gig. At the same time, David was in transition going from where he was with Ziggy to a whole other level of stardom. It was a pivotal point in both of our lives. When you go through something like that with somebody, the experience creates a bond that's hard to break and never really goes away, like having been in the trenches of a war together, or with the guys you got sober with. What can I say? Our relationship lasted through all the bullshit.

With former Sex Pistol, and my good friend, Glen Matlock.

Epilogue: The Slick Philosophy

In early 2020, I toured around with my good buddy, former Sex Pistol Glen Matlock.

One night, after 'Pretty Vacant', we finished the set with a cover of 'All or Nothing' by the Small Faces. Great song. I put the Sunburst Gibson Firebird I'd played through the tour back on the stand, jumped down from the stage and made my way through the crowd to the dressing room. It had been great to be back at the 100 Club with Glen. He'd played there back in 1976 with the Pistols, who were just one of a long list of greats who'd played the legendary London venue. Over the years, the 100 Club had seen heroes of mine like Muddy Waters, B. B. King, Chuck Berry, Buddy Guy, Jimi Hendrix, The Who, The Kinks and the Stones. And I'm just scratching the surface.

That was reason enough to soak up the atmosphere in the little basement club, but if I'd known that it was going to be the last time I played live for nearly two years, I'd have tried a little harder.

A week after we played the 100 Club, the world locked its doors when the pandemic hit and I got myself home to upstate New York. The next couple of years were a good time to reflect. I think we all did that.

Who would've thought, when I was a kid, that I'd end up working as a guitar slinger for a living, playing with so many of those heroes of mine who'd played the 100 Club before me. Even David had played there, aged just eighteen, in 1965, when he unveiled a new song, 'Can't Help Thinking About Me', which was then put away for thirty-five years until I rejoined his band in 1999 and we re-recorded it for *Toy*.

I had no agenda when I set out copying guitar parts off a record player as a kid, but somehow, whether it was just a session or two, a concert here or there, or a long-term partnership, I've had contact with most of them.

When I started working on this book, I made a list of my childhood heroes that I'd crossed paths with. I thought, looky there, I've got Keith Richards, Mick Jagger, John Lennon, George Harrison, Ringo Starr, Chuck Berry, Buddy Guy, plus a load of other people that I've gotten to know and gotten to work with. None of that was planned. I never chased any of them. I never initiated any of those relationships. It just seemed to happen. I must have been doing something right.

There were frustrations along the way, for sure. I certainly managed to lose a lot of guitars en route. And there were the nearlys and what ifs. There were disappointments galore. Sometimes just dumb luck, sometimes nobody's fault but mine. I had glimpses of what it was like to step into the limelight. A hit single or two and an MTV rotation in the eighties with Phantom, Rocker & Slick. But mostly, I was content to be working and getting gigs for what I could bring to the party. And I had the good fortune to hook up with David and John Lennon and leave my mark on one or two stone-cold classics.

The inside sleeve of *Station to Station*, it's always going to say: GUITAREARLSLICK.

Not bad for a guy with no Plan B.

I'll take it. No doubt about it, I've been one fortunate motherfucker and it's sure been a cool ride. So, my philosophy? Do what you love, never give up, and fuck the Plan B.

Tools of the Trade

When I started out, I approached the guitar the same way Keith Richards approached it, and that never changed. The tools of the trade – the guitars, amps, pedals and whatnot – have changed over the years, there's no doubt about that, but my approach never really varied all that much, although it certainly became more refined.

Pretty soon I started to know what I liked and what I didn't like. I'd walk into a guitar store and see fifteen or twenty or even thirty guitars, but I'd home in on just one, because I almost instinctively knew it was the right one for me.

The Danelectro Convertible

The first time I saw the Stones, right away I zoned in on Brian Jones and Keith Richards. In fact, at first I was more of a Brian fan. But after I'd seen the band on TV three or four times, it was all Keith as far as I was concerned. There was something that he had that I wanted, man. Badly. In short order, I started hammering on my old man to get me a guitar, because I hadn't had any real job yet. I beat the shit out of him, pestering him night and day, and he finally got me my first guitar, which was a Danelectro.

The guitar had a beige Formica top and white on the

sides. It was a double cutaway, and it had a sound hole. And on each side of the sound hole was a chrome button, about a half-inch across maybe. Where there would normally be tone controls and volume controls there were little silver grommets stuck into the guitar, with the idea that when you got good enough, you bought a kit and you could slide in a pickup and these knobs, and voila, you'd graduated to the electric guitar. I never did that though. But that's the guitar I learned to play on.

The Hagstrom II

When I was ready to get a real electric guitar, I bought a Hagstrom II. It was black and had this silvery-white raised pick guard, and all these little buttons everywhere. It looked cool, but mainly I got it because it was cheaper than any of the Fenders I wanted and I didn't have that kind of money.

I bought what was called *The Beatles' Second Album*, which came out here but was never an album in the UK, and that entire summer was spent in front of a record player with my guitar, working out how to play every song, top to bottom. I didn't have that Hagstrom for very long, though. I needed better gear.

The Fender Telecaster / Fender Deluxe Amplifier

I remember playing along with the Yardbirds' 'Heart Full of Soul' all the time, and seeing a Fender Telecaster in Jeff

Beck's hands on TV, and that became my next mission. I don't remember how long it took, but I saved up some money, took my Hagstrom, and went to Silver & Horland Music Store on Park Row, right across from City Hall in Manhattan. It's long gone, but I traded the Hagstrom in and got a 1065 Fender Telecaster. Including the trade-in, the guitar came to $125. They probably gave me $30 for that Hagstrom, but it was worth it to me because I loved that Telecaster. In fact, I still play Teles to this day. Pretty soon after that I bought an early 1960s 'blackface' Fender Deluxe amplifier for $80 from a listing I found in the newspaper. Eventually I got a Maestro Fuzz-Tone, too, but that was it. That was my setup for a really long time.

My First Real Rig

Mack Truck was my first real band. I was 16, and we were out there, all the time, working and making money. That's when I got my first Marshall amp. Because there was a band in Brooklyn called Dust. The drummer was a guy named Marc Bell and the bass player was Kenny Aaronson, who serious fans will know as one of the greats of the last forty years. They had a left-handed guitar player that played a Tele through a full stack, and holy shit. I didn't have the money for a stack, so I bought an eight-by-ten combo and a 50-watt head. And I switched from my Tele, and I got an SG, because that's what Eric Clapton was playing in Cream, who I loved. That was my first real rig.

Pedals

Over the years I've had Gibson SGs and Les Pauls but still – even with David – I never used a whole lot of pedals. I started off with a very 1960s mindset towards playing the guitar, which was really a throwback to the 1950s – you simply got yourself a good, reliable guitar and the loudest amp you could afford, and that was that. Like Keith, I developed the mindset over the years of needing my feet to walk, not stomp pedals, even if he did kick the whole pedal craze into high gear with 'Satisfaction'. None of us knew what a pedal was until that. But pretty soon we figured out that he'd used something call a Maestro Fuzz-Tone – a small, metal box with some knobs on it that you plugged your guitar into, and then plugged the other end into your amp – and we were all off to the races to find the newest and coolest sounds we could. Over the years, of course, like anything, guitar players of all stripes blew the use of pedals all out of proportion, but now most of us are back to pretty simple setups again.

Eventually I graduated to a Marshall amplifier loaded with Electro-Voice 200-watt speakers live for big gigs, with a Les Paul, or sometimes Fender Stratocaster-type guitars. And when the eighties arrived I did add some pedals, like for the Serious Moonlight Tour – a delay, a flanger and a boost pedal, so not really much. I was still using Marshalls, although I was playing custom-made DiMarzio Strats – which just had one DiMarzio X2N® pickup in it without a tone control, just a volume knob, and a Kahler vibrato – because I was a victim of the same awful gear choices that every guitar player in that era was guilty of.

The Gibson J-45

As far as acoustic guitars go, I've always played Gibsons. Always. My first acoustic was a 1968 Gibson J-45, and I still have it and use it on just about everything I do. I bought it new, and that's the guitar that I used on every one of the hit records I played on back in the day. In fact, it's the one that, after we finished recording *Young Americans*, David's 1975 hit album, he borrowed it and didn't give it back for what seemed like forever. It was so long – and I loved that guitar so much – that I started to panic. I was thinking, 'Who knows what happened to that guitar?' Eventually, I got it back from him. But it was something like six months later! And I didn't notice for a while, but there was a very small crack right below the headstock. I realized that I didn't get it back right away because he'd broken it, and he'd gotten it fixed, and that took a bit. And of course he didn't say anything!

But whoever fixed the guitar, which was back in 1975, did an amazing job. So it couldn't have been that bad, and whoever did the repair, it was fixed properly. And it's still perfect.

It always comes down to the Gibsons as far as acoustics go. I have other acoustic guitars and I play them, but when push comes to shove on a record, nine times out of ten it's going to be a Gibson. They have a particular sound, especially recorded. But it's not even about what's better, because I know guys that are strictly Martin guys, or Collings guys, or Taylor guys, which are made by a company out of Texas and have become very popular. But for me it's always been my Gibson J-45, that to this day just sounds great.

The SG Junior

I bought my trusty '65 Gibson SG Junior from a guy named Joe who worked at Sam Ash, a real big dude, who was *the* guy to deal with. I asked him for an SG Junior, and he told me that Gibson had stopped making them, but then said, 'Lemme see what I can find.' He went in the back and he came back with a brand new guitar. Because in those days guitars didn't fly out off the shelves, so you could have a two- or three-year-old brand-new guitar sitting there.

And that's the guitar I used on *David Live* at the Tower. In fact, it's the only guitar I actually owned at the time! If I broke a string, I'd use David's early-seventies Gibson Les Paul Black Beauty, which had three pickups. That was my spare. But I almost never used it, because my favourite was the SG, which was also used on all the early Bowie recordings I did, like *Young Americans*. As a matter of fact, that was the *only* guitar I used on that album, other than my Gibson J-45.

I've still got both of those guitars, too, which is weird, considering how many guitars have passed through my hands over the years. The SG has been repainted – it was

SG red and now it's turquoise blue, due to an attack of too much 1980s – and the pickup configuration was changed, so that needs to be put back to the way it was, which I intend to do one day. But the neck is still straight as an arrow and everything else is still there, just as it was in 1974. I do need to get it restored, because I love that guitar, and it's an important one.

As for that paint job, I had played that guitar so much that part of the finish was down to the wood. Nowadays people pay a lot of money for guitars that look like that, but back then I thought, 'Aww man, look at this thing. It's old and worn out, but I don't want to sell it.' Anyway, like I said, too much blow and the eighties combined made for a bad decision.

Originally, the guitar had one P-90 pickup and one of those really crappy vibrato arms on it. I ended up putting a Tune-o-Matic bridge on it, and by the time of *David Live* I'd already dropped some DiMarzio humbuckers in it.

It was even used on *Double Fantasy*. As a matter of fact, I remember that after the last day that we recorded with John, and I was ready to fly back to LA where I was living, I got a phone call first thing in the morning saying, 'Hold off. John's got something for you to do.' So they changed my ticket, and I headed over to the studio with my SG.

When I arrived, John told me he had this idea, with the two of us playing the solo in unison. And I remember it distinctly, because of the way we recorded it. We had two little baby Fender amps with a stereo mic between them, and we were facing each other, about three feet apart, and it was over this one line that he kept singing over and over again, 'I don't wanna face it,' which was also the title of the song. So I was playing my SG, while John was playing his Sardonyx guitar. And that was the version that ended up on the *Milk and Honey* record, but not the outtakes on the *John Lennon Anthology* boxset, which were live takes from the sessions.

So that SG was on *Double Fantasy, Milk and Honey,* Yoko's *Season of Glass, David Live, Station To Station, Young Americans* and lots of other recordings, and obviously means a lot to me.

The Fender Stratocaster

On *Station to Station* I mostly used my SG, a 1970 Les Paul Custom, and a 1962 Fender Stratocaster. Somebody had painted it purplish, and it had a bizarre stainless steel pick guard on it. It was an ugly fucking guitar, but it was a great guitar. And anytime you hear a whammy bar or feedback on 'Station' – and that's a lot, let's face it – it's that guitar.

With Ian Hunter, when we did the *Overnight Angels* record, I still had my 1962 Strat, so I was using that, as well as my SG and a Les Paul – those would've been the three main guitars, along with my J-45 acoustic – through a 100-watt Marshall half stack.

When we were recording the record, at home we had a crazy situation with a fire, but luckily my SG and the other guitars were at the studio, so the only guitars I had with me in the house that burned down were two Strats, a '64 and a

'62, both of which I was using on that album, actually. So, they were gone.

Setups for John and Yoko

On *Double Fantasy*, I used a combination of guitars, but mostly my Les Paul and the SG. Those were really my go-to guitars, as always through a Marshall. Plus, my J-45 and John's 'dragon' Yamaha acoustic, of course. On *Season of Glass*, I used the same setup. The only difference was that I brought my 1960s Vox AC30 amplifier with me, along with my Marshall. Not too long after those sessions, though, that AC30 was destroyed. My equipment didn't have a lot of luck around that time.

The Modified Longhorn

During the Phantom, Rocker and Slick days, Lee Rocker used a Danelectro Longhorn bass, and he had a Longhorn guitar, too, which he gave to me. Or at least that's how I understood it at the time. So I modified it, of course, because in the eighties, everything was up for modification. Carve it up; tear it apart; even if you didn't know why you were doing it. I can put some of it down to too much blow and my brain not working.

Unfortunately, I wasn't told until later that it was Jeff Baxter's guitar and he was none too happy about the modifications. I ended up giving it back to him, but then I was pissed. I was thinking, 'Wait a minute, nobody told me I had to give the guitar back!' Of course, maybe they did and I didn't hear them, but it was an uncomfortable situation, to say the least. And for years after that, I avoided Baxter like the plague, just being an asshole about it. Years later, when we'd run into each other, it was a laugh. But at the time, man, I was pissed.

As for some of my guitar choices and the amps I was using around that time, I really am not sure. I was just too high.

The Peaveys

In the early nineties, Peavey came to me to endorse their products. The guitars were actually good, but there wasn't anything I'd play. They asked me what I wanted, and they did have a guitar that was basically a Tele, so I had them do a mod paint job – real retro, 1950s red with the cream binding and a toilet seat pickguard – and added DiMarzio overwound Tele pickups, one guitar with a Bigsby tremolo and one without, and I really loved those guitars.

When David called me, I still had those Peaveys, as well as my SG and my J-45, though I'd sold just about everything else when I left the business in 1994. So that's what I came back into David's band with. Those early gigs back with him – Glastonbury and the BBC Theatre special and all that – that's all I had.

The Ones That Got Away

When we started to record *Toy*, David said, 'You know, Slick, I miss you with your Les Paul.' At that point Gibson was tying in with some of the guys in the band anyway, so I went and got a Les Paul, which I actually didn't use on *Toy*, or even the couple of tracks I played on for *Heathen*. But on *Reality*, that's for the most part a Custom Shop Les Paul. There were two of them. There was a black one and then there was a cherry burst. Sadly, they were stolen in 2008.

Long after David had stopped touring, I went to Canada to do a gig, and stayed there for a week or two. Instead of driving my own car, I rented a car, because it didn't have tinted windows or anything, and because I wanted to be able to put the guitars in the trunk, in case I had to stop at a rest stop. I thought I was pretty smart, hiring the most inconspicuous car on the planet. Somewhere after I'd crossed the border back into the States after the gig, they were stolen. The guitars were definitely in there, because the customs guys had made me open the trunk, but when I got home and started to unpack, the trunk was fucking empty. I remember standing there looking at the trunk for what seemed like forever, waiting for them to reappear. I'd been very cautious about where I stopped, and how long I went into the rest stops, which I'd only done a couple of times. But at one of the stops, somebody must have gotten into that trunk. What got me was that they'd done it without breaking into the car.

When I went to the cops, they said thieves at truck stops were becoming a rampant problem. They were getting those clickers, like what you use to get into your car, with a whole bunch of different frequencies, and they would just keep going around a parking lot until one of the cars popped open. So them getting those guitars – which I'd played all over the world on David's Reality Tour – was totally random! They had no idea what they had. Some dumb fuck probably sold those guitars for 100 bucks!

The Later Bowie Setup

I also got a Gibson Double Cutaway Goldtop Les Paul, with a chambered body, which I used on *Reality*, along with a black ESP Ronnie Wood Telecaster and a black ESP Stratocaster with DiMarzio Strat pickups in it. I also met this guy in Philadelphia who had a place called DiPinto Guitars, which was a tiny little storefront shop. His guitars were retro, sparkly, gaudy-looking things, but they sounded good, so I ended up buying one and I used it on one song during that last tour with David, 'Diamond Dogs'.

I had also gotten a really nice Epiphone 335 with a Bigsby on it. It was a new one – not vintage – and I'd put some DiMarzio humbuckers in it and rewired it, so it was a great guitar. In my first days back with David I wasn't using an Ebow yet – a gizmo that you hold above the strings of the guitar to create endless sustain – so on 'Heroes' I was using the 335, which is a hollow-bodied guitar, getting the feedback I needed. I was able to control it because those guitars are almost made to feed back.

As for amps, I was using late-nineties Ampeg Reverberocket half stacks that I picked up at Chicago Music Exchange. In fact, I ended up selling those amps for whatever reason, and I really missed them, so I found another one, just by chance, again at Chicago Music Exchange, in 2018 and I bought it. I got it when we were out on the road with the Garson band.

I also had a deal with Line 6 by then, so I was using a Line 6 delay pedal – the big green one, if you're keeping track – for the backwards stuff I had to do on 'I'm Afraid of Americans' and whatever else. I also had a Boss stereo digital delay and a Boss flanger, as well as their green Tube Screamer, which I really only used occasionally. It wasn't my favourite pedal, and when we got to *Reality*, I bought a fuzz tone, which I liked much better and used on the title track. There's a very gnarly sound on there, too. I ran the Pod into my amp to get that. That fuzz sound is coming out of a Pod in combination with the fuzz tone.

During the *Reality* period, I didn't bring out my old SG, so I was pretty much using Les Pauls onstage. Occasionally, on the tunes I would need them on, like the beginning of 'Station to Station', I played my ESP Strat, as well as a Gibson J-200 acoustic and a Tacoma 12-string acoustic.

I worked on *The Next Day* in July of 2012, so I was still primarily using my Framus signature model, the red one with the two DiMarzio P-90s and a Bigsby on it. And by that point I'd stopped bringing my J-45 to the studio, so I used a Gibson 75th anniversary mini J-200 on that record, when I needed to lay down any acoustics David had in mind.

I'd bought some amps from Orange, so that was primarily what I used. It was an Orange 30-watt head and two two-by-twelve cabinets with Celestian Golds.

My Current Rig

As for my current setup, I can thank Bill Nash for that. I was at NAMM in 2010, at the booth for the resurrected Magnavox brand of amps, and as I was sitting there testing the amps out, the guy manning the booth, who turned out to be the owner of the company, handed me a Telecaster. I picked that guitar up and said, to no one in particular, 'Wow. What is this thing and who made it?' And a voice chimed in from behind me, saying, 'I did.'

It was Bill Nash. He introduced himself and asked, 'Do you want one?' I couldn't get the words 'I'd love one' out fast enough. So Bill built me one of his Nash Telecasters – and I loved it so much that I got another one not long after that – and those have been my main guitars for a good ten years now. I'd gone full circle. Bill's guitars inspired me. And it was funny, because the guitar I coveted and felt the most comfortable with at the beginning, is the same one that I'm using now, and have been for quite a while.

And somewhere around the late nineties, Ampeg started making an amp called the Reverberocket. It's a 50-watt half stack amplifier, but it's got nothing to do with the original Reverberocket amps from the sixties, other than the name.

But they're amazing, and those are the amps I used on all of the 2000 Bowie tours. All of them. I still have one and use it, along with a '59 reissue Fender Bassman amp and a Fender Blues Junior, as well as a Marshall Studio MKII, which are all great amps with my Teles. So I'm back to using not just a Telecaster, but old-school sixties amps, too.

DiMarzio Pickups

My relationship with DiMarzio pickups goes back to – my God – 1970! Larry DiMarzio was one of the best luthiers in Manhattan. He worked at Eddie Bell's guitar shop, and I would take my guitars there for repairs and whatever. And as the relationship formed – because I was a pretty steady customer – I would talk to him about the gigs that I was doing, and how I kept getting fired because I didn't really like to use fuzz tones, and I wanted my amp to break up but, of course, I refused to use anything smaller than a 100-watt Marshall, so I was just too damn loud for everyone.

One day, he said, 'I can do something with the pickups that might help break that amp up a little bit quicker.' So he did. He took the pickups out of my SG and he rewound them, to make them sound fatter, and louder. And as time went on, because I did a lot of gigs back then – even before working with David Bowie I was doing four or five gigs a week in the early seventies – a lot of the other guitar players that came to see what I was up to, because there was healthy competition, were knocked out by my guitar sound.

I was getting questions about how I was getting the sound and I told them all, 'This guy, Larry DiMarzio, he's really got this down.' Over time, Larry started doing the same modifications for other people. One thing led to another, and eventually he figured, 'Why am I doing this? I should be making my own pickups.' And that's what happened.

The Earl Slick Model

I met the guy who ran Framus guitars, H. P. Wilfer, through Dwight Devereaux at TonePro. I had already endorsed TonePro for their guitar hardware, and was at the Germany Musikmesse, which is their NAMM. Dwight is a good guy, and his company is very high-profile, even though it still feels like a family-run business.

Anyway, Dwight from TonePro introduced me to H. P. Wilfer, whose father formed Framus in the late 1940s. It had gone bankrupt, but eventually, through his success with Warwick basses, H. P. was able to resurrect Framus. When we met, I was really interested. I loved the guitars. He offered to make an Earl Slick signature model, and I was thrilled. As a prototype, I used a model that he had from the 1960s, and then I went from there and designed what turned out to be the Framus Earl Slick model. From that moment on, we've had a great relationship all the way.

Acknowledgements

I want to acknowledge everyone I've worked with. You know who you are. I could not have had this amazing career without you. I want to especially thank those who made this book possible:

Jeff Slate, for hanging in there for all the hours. You helped me tell the story that I didn't know I had in me.

Rowland White, for his dedication and vision for the book, and Ruth Atkins, for her able and necessary support, as well as the team at Michael Joseph and Penguin Random House UK, including Helen Eka, Nick Lowndes, Stella Newing, Lauren Wakefield, Lee Motley, Alice Chandler, Ellie Hughes, Mubarak Elmubarak, Nicola Evans and Christina Ellicott.

My literary agent, Lynn Johnston, for expert guidance and sound judgement. Also thanks to Sandy Hodgman, for help with foreign sales.

Jennifer M. Kennedy, for getting the ball rolling.

Glen Matlock, for keeping me sane during the pandemic.

Francis Whately, for putting together and directing my 'Rock and Roll Guns for Hire'.

Slim Jim Phantom and Lee Rocker, for being the only band that gave me a top ten hit.

Joe Elliot and Robert Smith, for giving me great songs.

John and Yoko, for being John and Yoko.

David Bowie, for the opportunity of a lifetime.

Finally, my kids, Marita, Lee and Cooper. I love you.

Discography

ALBUMS

2023 *Fist Full of Devils*
2003 *Zig Zag*
2000 *Lost and Found*
2001 *Live 1976*
2002 *Slick Trax*
1991 *In Your Face*
1976 *Razor Sharp*
1976 *Earl Slick Band*

Selected work with others

with David Bowie

TOY:BOX (2022)
I'm Only Dancing (The Soul Tour 74) (2020)
Serious Moonlight (live, 1983) (2019)
Glastonbury 2000 (2018)
Cracked Actor (Live Los Angeles '74) (2017)
The Next Day (2013)
A Reality Tour (2004)
Reality (2003)
Heathen (2002)

Bowie at the Beeb: The Best of the BBC Radio Sessions 68–72
   (2000)
Ziggy Stardust: The Motion Picture (1983) (Uncredited overdubs)
Station To Station (1976)
Young Americans (1975)
David Live (1974)
Diamond Dogs (1974) (Uncredited)
Rare (1972)

with John Lennon & Yoko Ono

Milk and Honey (1984)
Double Fantasy (1980)

with Yoko Ono

Season of Glass (1981)

with Phantom Rocker & Slick

Cover Girl (1986)
Phantom, Rocker & Slick (1985)

SELECTED CREDITS

2024   *The Last Day of Summer*, Jeff Slate
2024   *KillerStar*, KillerStar
2023   *Consequences Coming*, Glen Matlock
2023   *Earl Slick and the West Side Social Club*, The Ripcords
2020   *Love Songs*, Whitesnake

2018   *Good to Go*, Glen Matlock

2017   *If Not Now Then When*, The Motels

2016   *Secret Poetry*, Jeff Slate

2015   *Love & Scars*, Jerry Gaskill,

2011   *Live from the Bowery 2011*, New York Dolls

2010   *Dreamtime*, Jeff Slate

2010   *Anik Jean*, Anik Jean

2009   *Another Year/Endless Flight*, Leo Sayer

2008   *Le Ciel Saigne le Martyre*, Anik Jean

2006   *Blue Suede Shoes: A Rockabilly Session*, Carl Perkins

2004   *A Forest (feat. Earl Slick, Unreleased 2001)*, The Cure,

2004   *A Tribute to Aerosmith*

2001   *Meet Joe Mac*, Joe Mac

2001   *Lynne Me Your Ears: A Tribute to the Music of Jeff Lynne*

2000   *Into the Light*, David Coverdale

1998   *This Time It's Different . . .* , Little Caesar

1997   *One Step Up/Two Steps Back: The Songs of Bruce
        Springsteen*

1992   *Influence*, Little Caesar

1991   *Hudson Hawk* (Original Motion Picture Sound-
        track*)*, Michael Kamen and Robert Kraft

1990   *Joe Cocker Live*, Joe Cocker

1990   *Bad Reputation*, Dirty White Boy

1989   *Junkyard*, Junkyard

1985   *Some People*, Belouis Some

1985   *Dancing in the Street*, David Bowie and Mick Jagger

1985   *Double Crossed*, Jim Diamond

1984   *Box of Frogs*, Box of Frogs

1982   *Suffer for Fashion*, Leroy Jones

1982   *Heart on a Wall*, Jimmy Destri

1981 *Silver Condor,* Silver Condor
1981 *Simplicity,* Tim Curry
1981 *Little Lost Girls,* The Runaways
1980 *Amerika,* Tonio K
1978 *Life in the Foodchain,* Tonio K
1978 *Ladies on the Stage,* Millington
1978 *And Now . . . The Runaways,* The Runaways
1977 *Overnight Angels,* Ian Hunter
1976 *Endless Flight,* Leo Sayer
1975 *Once Bitten Twice Shy,* Ian Hunter
1972 *Even a Broken Clock Is Right Twice a Day,* Tracks

Index